T0195857

FIVE
LIFE LESSONS
FROM THE
AKASHIC
RECORDS

TAPPING INTO THE MEMORIES OF GOD

DR. YANA MILEVA

BALBOA.PRESS
A DIVISION OF HAY HOUSE

Balboa Press books may be ordered through booksellers or by contacting:

Balboa Press
A Division of Hay House
1663 Liberty Drive
Bloomington, IN 47403
www.balboapress.com
844-682-1282

Print information available on the last page.

ISBN: 979-8-7652-2970-5 (sc)
ISBN: 979-8-7652-2972-9 (hc)
ISBN: 979-8-7652-2971-2 (e)

Library of Congress Control Number: 2022911988

Balboa Press rev. date: 08/16/2022

To all the people in my life who continuously teach me what unconditional love means.

CONTENTS

FOREWORD

This book offers the reader a powerful and practical guide for all areas of life. The heartfelt stories are truly touching because they show the reader the relationship between the problem in one's awareness while simultaneously shedding light on the underlying root issues. Because of this correlation, the heart opens easily and touches our core being. Thank you, Yana, for this wonderful work!

—Rev. Gabrielle Orr, author of *Akashic Records, One True Love*; *Let Miracles Happen: Understanding Your Own Power with Help of The Akashic Records*; and *Akasha-Chronik Orakel—You Are Loved*

ACKNOWLEDGMENTS

I started working with the Akashic records in year 2010. The first time I entered the records, the masters immediately started talking to me, even without me asking them a question. My teacher, Maureen J. St. Germain, told me, "They have been waiting for a long time to connect with you and have a lot to tell you now."

I am extremely grateful to every single person who supported and guided me on my path. I would like to especially thank my earthly teachers in the Akashic records, in their order of appearance: Maureen J. St. Germain, Gabrielle Orr, Milush Kadiev, Athena Santoriniou, and Ernesto Ortiz. My life would not be the same without you. You have my eternal love and gratitude.

I would like to particularly thank Gabrielle Orr for believing in me and for showing me how to teach the knowledge of the Akashic records to others. You helped one of my biggest dreams and my soul purpose come to life. Thank you.

PREFACE

You are holding in your hands a book that contains the sacred wisdom of the Akashic records. This book is a collection of my personal experiences with the records, as well as experiences I had with my clients throughout the years.

Before I introduce the Akashic records to you, let me first introduce myself. I was born in Bulgaria, in the family of two mathematics teachers. My parents loved me and did everything they could to provide a good life for me. I spent every summer break at the farmhouse of my grandparents and was surrounded by my big, happy family. But despite all the loving people around me, I felt lonely. Even as a child, I somehow knew that there must be more to life than what I was told. I said once to my mother, "I believe I was born with a purpose! I just do not yet know what it is, but I feel that it is something big!" My mother looked at me and said something that surprised me at that moment but that now I very well understand. She said, "Everyone has this feeling." So, I kept looking for my purpose and for this thing that would give meaning to my life.

One day, the book *Linda Goodman's Sun Signs*, of the famous American astrologist Linda Goodman, landed in our home. I didn't leave it until I had read every single word of it. And then I did the same with her other books. My entire family was obsessed with astrology for an entire year! One of Linda Goodman's books I read many times—*Star Signs: The Secret Codes of the Universe*. This book opened doors for me that never closed. I realized that there was indeed much more to life than what modern society tells us. And I started reading one book after another, looking for answers to all the questions swirling in my head. While girls my age were busy learning how to apply makeup (I have to admit, I still struggle with this), I was learning about the earth's lay lines, the pyramids, the crop circles, and the secrets of Mount Kailash. Each book answered some of my current questions but also sprouted new ones. So, I kept on searching for *the* book that would hold the answers to all my questions. And one day I found it. It was the Book of Life—the Akashic records. It was not the paper book I expected it to be, but it was the book that I had been craving to find my entire life. And now, with this book you hold, I hope to offer you the answers to some of the biggest life questions you might have. Enjoy the ride!

In the first chapter, you will learn what the Akashic records are and who the masters and teachers of the records are. I thought I learned about the existence of the Akashic records when I was twenty-seven years old. However, the masters and teachers told me years later that we had been in contact from a lot earlier. They told me they were the wind that played with my hair when I was a child; they were the soft, loving voice in my ears when I thought I was alone; and they were the ever-present, gentle, loving embrace when I was falling asleep. So you see, your story is probably similar to mine. Maybe you think you are opening for the first time a book about the Akashic records, but in reality, you already know the contents of this and of many other books. So, thank you for the opportunity to remind you of what your soul already knows and to urge you in the direction you have always wanted to explore. The moment each one of us starts following our soul's purpose, this world will be filled with much happier and fulfilled people. We have the potential to turn our lives into blessed heaven or a living hell, so let us choose together to call back the heaven here on earth.

In the second chapter, you will find a collection of the most frequently asked questions by my clients and the corresponding answers, as given by the masters. If you have an area in your life that you would like to bring to the next level, the information in this chapter can support you in this. Here you will find the life lessons that each one of us needs to learn in order to live a happy and fulfilling life.

In the third chapter, I share ten real-life readings from my coaching practice. To preserve the privacy of my clients, I changed their names in the stories, as well as other personal details. The specific information received from the records is sacred and is only for the affected person to know. However, the masters have allowed selected readings to be shared in this book, as spreading the wisdom of these readings can help more than one person. The information from the Akashic records has the potential to solve mysteries we have been facing our entire life—within minutes. I know no other tool that aims so precisely and transforms us so gently but quickly and with so much love and compassion.

The fourth chapter is dedicated to channeled answers from the Akashic records. I connect to the records on a daily basis and have asked many, many questions throughout the years. This chapter is a collection of some of the questions I have posed to the masters, as well as to God him/herself.

I hope the stories in this book will help you come a step (or two or ten) closer to the ultimate knowledge of the universe and that it will support your soul in achieving its goals. The contact with the Akashic records has taught me how to be more myself, how to love and not to judge, and how to understand people and life. The transformation in me has been quiet but steady, slow at first glance but enormous in retrospect. This is how the Akashic field and the masters and teachers from the Akashic records work with us—at our own pace, with love, patience, and tons of understanding. Regardless of our actions or decisions, we will always be loved, no matter what—loved by the masters and loved by God, unconditionally.

Let me quickly clarify one thing before we continue. In this book, you will stumble across the word *God* quite often. For simplicity, I will address him/her with him, but of course, God does not have a gender. Other synonyms for God, which you will see throughout the book, are source, universe, creator, and all-that-is. I am not using any of these words in a religious context. I grew up in a communist country where religion was not part of society, so I am not indoctrinated by the church terms. Even when I was in my early twenties and I moved to Germany, I was shocked that so many people there believed in God. I was convinced that every well-educated, modern person knows that God does not exist; it was like the story of Santa Claus—simply a nice story people enjoyed. Of course, when I started working with the Akashic records, my ideas about God changed. For me now and for a lack of a better term, "God" means all-that-is, the beginning and the end of all, the original source—not a vindictive old chap with a white beard, sitting on a cloud, whom we need to fear. I am using the word *God* because I do not have a better one to describe the energy that birthed us all, the energy that has endless love for us, the energy that always has us in its embrace. If you have another word to describe it, feel free to use that word instead. We are all only humans, and grasping the ideas of infinity, endlessness, timelessness, unconditional love, or simply the scale of the universe is mind-boggling. And yet we do not need to understand it with our minds in order to feel it and understand it with our hearts.

Throughout the book, you will see that I also often speak of the masters, teachers, and lords of the Akashic records. Just as we are found on the earth plane, on the plane of the Akashic records, these beings are found. The masters are those who have mastered unconditional love. The teachers are those among them who took over the task of teaching the rest of the beings in the universe how to also master unconditional love. The lords of the Akashic records are those who are taking care of the records and making sure that no one gets access to information that is not for him/her to know. You can imagine them as the caretakers, the librarians, or the security guards in the galactic library of the Akashic records.

If you can already access the Akashic records, this book will give you great ideas about your own development and spiritual work. If you have not yet been consciously in contact with the Akashic records, I urge you to establish this connection as soon as possible. The stage is set for you. It is no coincidence you are holding this book now. Maybe this is preparing you for the next step—the actual connection to the Akashic field. Many events in your life led you to this moment, so do not take it lightly. If you are interested in learning how to channel from the Akashic records, feel free to visit my website https://joyridecoaching.com. There you will find listed books and seminars that can teach you this invaluable skill. My goal with this book is to open the door to the land of wonders for you and convince you to go through it. In the process, I would like to prepare you for what awaits you and give you some first-aid tools that will assist you in mastering your life. I have selected the most important lessons that repeat again and again in the Akashic records sessions I give. They have served me, and they served my clients, and I am sure they will serve you too. And now sit back, enjoy the ride, and turn to the next page of this book … and the next chapter of your life.

Thousands of candles can be lit from a single candle, and the life of the candle will not be shortened. Happiness never decreases by being shared. (Buddha)

CHAPTER 1

The Akashic Records

You can search throughout the entire universe for someone who is more deserving of your love and affection than you are yourself, and that person is not to be found anywhere. You, yourself, as much as anybody in the entire universe, deserve your love and affection.
—Buddha

The Akashic records are the memory of God. They contain, among other things, the information of what has happened in our universe, what is happening right now, and what could happen in the future. The future is not carved in stone. I know—shocking, right? But this is actually very good news, as you will later see.

When I first entered the Akashic records, I felt an overwhelming warm feeling of finally being home. In this moment, I did not need anything else in life. I was loved; I was safe; I was home, and all was good and perfect. All my earthly problems felt suddenly so small and insignificant. My trip and my search for answers had finally come to an end. I did not need anything else anymore. Everything paled in comparison to the cosmic love that waited for me in the records. This is the love we have all been craving, and looking for, and dying for, and killing for, and doing all the right and all the wrong things for. And it was never there where we searched for it, but it has always been right here in front of us. We just have to open the correct door.

The Akashic records have had many names throughout history. One of the most famous ones is the Book of Life. As a result of this, many people think that the Akashic records are a library or a book in the sky from which we can read written texts. And who writes these texts? Did God do it? Did our soul do it? In truth, the Akashic records are simply an energetic imprint of all this that has been, of all this that currently is, and of all this that is to (maybe) come. They are a dynamic energy field that is different in every moment of existence, because when we change, it changes with us. Our fate is not written in a book, and neither we nor God has prewritten it. What God *wrote* are the rules of the game: "Be a creator, have free will, love is the strongest energy, go explore if you wish, but come back home to me." How the actual game develops is up to the players; it is up to us.

So, if you think your future is written on the pages of a big book up in the sky, think again. I am sorry to disappoint you, but your fate lies fully in your hands. This can sometimes be quite frustrating because it means we have no one else to blame for the life we have but ourselves. However, blame is the last thing you will find in the records. Or rather, it is nowhere to be found in the records. Love does not blame. Love loves.

Having said that, you need to know that while you have free will, your soul has free will too. What does this mean? It means that your soul chose for you—for this current incarnation of its own—the frames of your current life. How you will move within these frames is your choice, but the frames are often already set. Your soul made a plan for what it (you) wants to experience and to check how well it can cope with the planned challenges and what lessons it (you) can learn. So next time, it (you) can achieve even more. The goal of life is life itself, and life always wants to grow and expand.

You can imagine your soul like a mountain climber. A person who wants to climb Mount Everest knows that he needs to prepare first. So such a person will put himself through some vigorous training in order to build the necessary stamina. Such a person will also put challenges in front of him so he can test himself as to how well prepared he really is for the real goal. If he notices that he lacks in some skill, he will plan to build that skill. The soul does the same. It challenges itself and selects the lessons it needs to achieve its goals.

And yet we do have the possibility within one lifetime to achieve enlightenment, to free ourselves completely of karma, and to fully ascend back to God—that is, to achieve all goals in one go. We *are* gifted with free will and having free will means we have the power to change everything. And by everything, I do mean *everything* within the boundaries of the existing universe. As we change, our actions change. And consequently, our future, and this, which is imprinted in the Akashic records, changes.

The bigger question is rather—are we ready to change and live the more expanded version of our life? If you are ready to catch the fast-track train, the masters and teachers of the Akashic records will be more than happy to support you. You are capable in every moment of completely rewriting your past, present, and future. The past, the present, and the future exist simultaneously, and thus by changing one aspect, you influence all other aspects of the time-space continuum. We can change the past. Think: the Mandela effect. We can change our future. Just take a different action next time you get the chance.

On earth, we have access to the present moment, and by influencing the present moment, we can change the past and the future. The Akashic records may assist you in this. You may look at the records like a storage of all the possible outcomes of all the possible situations throughout time and space. So, working with the masters and teachers of the records, you can have them direct you into the scenario, into the reality you most desire. But do not get fooled. This is your life, and you need to take the necessary actions in order to see the transformations you crave.

Knowing what to do, however, does not mean it will be easy to do it or it will be a quick fix for life. The light beings in the records can only direct us, guide us, and give us their love. They cannot—and do not want to—live our lives instead of us. I have wished many times for the masters to fix my life with a magic wand, but unfortunately (or fortunately), they would never do such a thing. This would be one of the biggest crimes in the universe—robbing a being of its free will and its experience of life.

Having the chance to live and play the game of life is the greatest gift we can receive from God. No one is permitted to take this away from us, not even the masters and teachers of the Akashic records. We personally made the conscious decision to come to earth. It was our decision to join the game of lower, material vibrational frequencies and risk getting into the cycle of reincarnation on earth. It was our decision to come here. So, by living in the confusion of duality, we learn to appreciate the good, the light, and the love so much more. You can imagine us like curious explorers who knew that some challenges might await them on the path but chose to take on this big adventure—called life—anyway because it is so worth experiencing. And no one returns home the same.

The Masters and Teachers in the Akashic Records

By now, you must be asking yourself, "Who are these masters and teachers really?" I am glad you asked.

I assume everyone reading this book will agree that we live on the planet Earth, and we reside in the 3-D dimension. We are aware of the fourth dimension—time—but we are not able to travel up and down its line at will. In a similar manner, there are beings that live on the higher dimension of the Akashic records. We call them masters, as these beings have achieved the highest level of craftsmanship in the universe and beyond. They have mastered the art of loving unconditionally and understand fully that they are sparks of God. Some of them we know under the term *ascended masters*. These are beings like Jesus Christ and Buddha. The ascended masters have walked a similar path to ours (incarnating on a lower, material plane of existence) and have ascended in one go from the lower dimensions straight up to the dimension of the Akashic records (the last dimension before the dimension of God). There are of course ascended masters who originate from different planets than ours, and we do not know (and cannot even pronounce) their names. However, the principle remains the same. To return to God, you can either directly ascend from where you are right now or take the longer (but maybe more fun) path of climbing step by step through the dimensions.

At the same time, just as there are beings, like us all, who chose to reincarnate on lower dimensions, there are also beings who never took on this adventure and have never incarnated in a physical dimension. Some of them are, for example, the archangels. The archangels have too much of an important role in the universe for them to squeeze down into a human body. They have been invited by God to come into existence and take over the specific tasks they are given. As they (and we all) are inseparable parts of God, his and their decisions and wishes are one and the same.

From all the masters, some chose the task of teaching the other beings in the universe and being closely involved with our soul growth. These beings we call our teachers. Here are a few examples of such teachers, whom you might meet in the Akashic records: Jesus Christ, Ganesha, Mother Mary, Buddha, archangel Michael, archangel Gabriel. I am sure at least some of these names are familiar to you. This should give you an idea of who is awaiting you in the records.

For every question and every need you have, a different being or a group of beings can greet you in the records and make sure you receive the most appropriate assistance on a case-by-case basis. I personally sometimes see individual masters, like Jesus, or some of the archangels, like archangel Gabriel. However, most of the time, I am communicating with a group of beings who are speaking as one voice to me. I often see them in a circle or sitting around a table, which of course is simply a way my brain is trying to process the energy in an understandable manner. But regardless of what and how you see, you will always feel the same when you communicate with the Akashic records—an endless stream of unconditional love, nonjudgment, and peace.

My Records versus Others' Records

Just like in any other self-respecting library, the information in the Akashic records is organized in a specific way and is guarded by wise librarians who make sure you get the right book or meet the right specialist for your needs. We call these librarians the lords of the Akashic records. No half-decent librarian will give a quantum physics book to a four-year-old child who cannot even properly read yet. Similarly, the Akashic records' librarians, who are much more than simply half-decent, make sure you get your hands on the most appropriate information for your soul age, knowledge level, and needs.

If I want to ask something about myself, or about the people in my life, or generally about the world, this information will come from the sections in the records that are relevant to me and to these questions. I will not be given access to other sections in the records because the contents there are not relevant for me and my questions. Similarly, if I am asked by a client in a session to access information in the records relevant for him or her, I will be given access to these corresponding sections of the Akashic records.

Who is requesting the information (me for myself or someone else through me) influences not only the sections of the library that I am allowed to access but also how this information will be presented. Depending on who is asking, the information will be presented in a manner that this specific person will understand best. The librarians of the records are quite the specialists at providing us exactly that which we need (even if we did not know we needed it).

What Kind of Information Can You Receive from the Akashic Records?

When in the Akashic records, we can ask questions and receive the information we need. This on its own is invaluable. Do you want to know how the universe came into existence? Do you want to know what kind of aliens are on other planets (or on ours)? Or maybe you would like to know the perfect food for you and your body. Or how to find your soul mate. All this information and a lot more can be found in the Akashic records.

One thing, however, that I explain to my clients when they come for the first time for a reading is that an Akashic records session is not fortune-telling. What people often wish to hear from the records (and what they rarely do hear) is specific information about their future. Questions like "When am I going to get married?" or "How long will I live?" or "Where should I invest my money?" rarely get the desired (or any) answers. The reason for this is that the masters simply do not know with 100 percent certainty what our future holds, because we are truly able to change our future in every single moment, and we often do. Fixating us on one probable future might be irresponsible and even detrimental; we might screen out other possibilities that are there for us and focus only on the one predicted future, in effect producing a self-fulfilling prophecy. The masters would have robbed us of the diversity of life and the freewill choice.

It is also possible that it simply does not serve us to know the answers to these questions (e.g., knowing when we will die). Usually, behind such future-related questions hides another kind of question—or rather deep desires or fears: "Please tell me I will get married soon." "Please tell me my child will be fine." "Please tell me what to do to be happy (I think I can achieve it by being rich)." Not many people really want to know the future when they go to a fortune-teller. What they really wish to hear is that their dreams will come true in the future. Thus, much better questions to ask in the records are "What do I need to know or do in order to find my ideal partner as soon as possible?"

or "What do I need to know or do in order to help my child live a long, happy life?" or "What do I need to know or do to have financial freedom?" Remember, there is not one fixed future for us. We are the masters of our lives and the creators of our personal universe.

The goal of the work with the records is to step into our own power; it is not to give the power of our life decisions into the hands of some almighty beings. The masters and teachers do not want to live our lives instead of us. They want to help us grow, blossom, and expand until we reach the limit of our potential, and this limit … is God himself. They are not interested in the future that holds the highest probability from the point in life we currently are at (what fortune-telling is); they are rather interested in telling us about our highest potential probability. The answers you receive from them will always point you toward your highest joy, because there lie the answers to all your prayers and to all the prayers of the universe.

An Akashic records session is not an "I sit and do nothing, and you give me information and save me" kind of an interaction. The consultant, client, and the masters and teachers come together with a common goal—to shift the life of all involved (led by the questions and problems of the client) a step, or more, further along the soul evolution path. If the person is willing to do the job (and if it serves his soul's plan), centuries-old karma can be resolved within minutes, old-time grudges can be forgiven, physical bodies can be transformed. It is a joined effort, not a one-man show where the consultant takes all the work and glory, the masters do some magic, and the client assumes the role of a damsel in distress who needs saving. None of us need saving. We are the masters of our lives, the captains of our life ships, and the rulers of our destiny. And this is how the masters and teachers in the Akashic records treat us.

One of the easiest ways to evaluate if a channeler is indeed connected to the records is the quality of the received information. If the information is coming from the masters, it will ring true in your ears. The words will resonate on a very deep soul level. Even if we do not have proof for the events the masters mention or do not fully comprehend the deeper meaning of their words, we somehow know they are true. For example, you might not remember your past lives (and might not be able to prove the mentioned events indeed occurred), but when the masters start telling you about a specific past-life experience and how it is linked to your current situation, you know deep in your core it is true because it does sound familiar to you. I sometimes channel from the records the most insane scenarios of a past life, and my clients say, "I knew it!"

Beside the deep truth in the received information, the other quality of the energy streaming to us from the Akashic records is the energy of unconditional love. No word is uttered from the records that is not in alignment with God's truth and unconditional love. You will never be judged, you will never be scolded, and you will never be blamed for anything you have ever done, either by the masters and teachers or by God. This is what unconditional love means—to be loved deeply and passionately, no matter what. I cannot stress this enough. We think we know what love means, but we mostly live in a world of very conditional love: "I will love you if you make me happy," "I will love you if you bring home good grades," "I will love you if you behave as I want you to behave." This is conditional love, because if we do not fulfill the given conditions of the love deal, we are threatened to lose the love. And there is nothing more terrifying to us than being left unloved and alone. I often hear "I do everything for him (a child, partner, friend), and he is still not happy!" But love should not be given to us because we earned it through our giving and serving. We do not want that; we often just don't know another way to get love. The true love we crave is unconditional; it does not depend on how much or less we give or do. We all remember what it feels to be loved that way. This is the memory of being one with God, and we all want to go back to this state. We yearn to be loved without requirements and expectations. All the wars and fighting in our world are simply a desperate attempt to find this love again. And this is why the words of the masters touch us on a very deep, emotional level and why they can heal us.

They come from a space of real unconditional love; they come from home. We have become masters of the fear-based and conditional love; what we need to master now is the art of unconditional love.

Receiving a reading from the Akashic records is a wonderful experience that has the potential to change your life forever. And as much as I love giving readings to my clients, exactly because of this potential, I urge everyone to learn for themselves how to connect with their own Akashic records. By communicating with the masters, we not only receive answers to our questions, but we also receive an energetic attunement. The love trickles down to us drop by drop (at a rate that is suitable for us) and awakens us to our own beauty and potential. By connecting to the masters, our energy and their energy become one. Our boundaries fall away, and we allow unconditional love and support to enter our lives and transform us. The more we interact with the masters, the more their energy rubs off of us and the higher our vibration becomes.

When we face the masters and the teachers in the records, we receive much more than their words—we sit in their presence and their aura. Jim Rohn once said that we are the average of the five people in our life that we spend the most time with; imagine who you will become when the masters and the teachers are part of your group of five. This is the biggest gift of the work with the Akashic records—your transformation on a deep energetic, psychological, and physical level. In actuality, the masters answer our questions just because we are asking and they like obliging us, but the real miracle that happens comes not so much from the information itself as from simply being in this field of high vibration. This contact serves as a catalyst for us to let go of any disharmonies in us and to come closer and closer to being one with God's truth and love.

The Akashic Records and Your Daily Life

When I first started working with the Akashic records, I wanted to keep the connection open all the time, so that at any moment, when I needed guidance, the information would be available to me.

This is not exactly what the masters want for us. They don't want us to be dependent on them; they want to teach us how to be our own guides. Funnily enough—or should I say, just as expected—the more I worked with the records, the more the energy of Akasha soaked into my being, and I started having more intuitive experiences and more synchronicities in my life (even when I was not consciously connected to the records). It became easier and easier for me to make my own decisions without having to ask the masters for advice first. The more you stay in the energy of the Akashic records, the more it becomes part of you. This is one of the most important things I learned from this work—the ability to navigate my life on my own.

In the beginning, when I learned how to consciously connect to the records, I had many questions, as I had many life situations about which I wasn't particularly happy. However, regardless of how many times I was asking the same question, the answer was still the same. No matter how often you ask, until you do your inner work, the answer will not change. Example: "Is this man for me? No? Really? Okay, I'll check tomorrow again." While I was working on transforming the different areas of my life, I still wanted to stay in daily contact with the Akashic records and had to come up with other questions I could ask on a regular basis. So, I thought, *What could be a question you can ask every day but receive a different answer worth giving?* Here are some example questions I came up with:

- What should my goals for today be?
- What does God want/expect from me today?
- What can I do to live my life to the fullest today, with most ease and joy?
- What would you like to tell me today? What would you like me to know?
- Why is this situation happening to me? How can I enjoy it to the fullest? What can I learn from it?
- What is the most loving thing to do in this situation? What would God do?

- Whom do I need to forgive?
- What did I learn today?
- What do I need to let go of from this day, so I can go to bed at peace and with a pure heart, body, and soul?

One of the greatest gifts you receive from the Akashic records is the ability to connect with them at any time and place. No matter where you are, no matter what your inner state of being is, if you need them, they are there for you. Especially when you are feeling lonely, sad, or angry—the moments when you need a hug, a loving word, some guidance—these are the best moments to connect to your Akashic records.

I went to a seminar once. I had to fly all the way from Germany to the USA for it, and I found myself in a place that was nice but also quite different from what I am used to. I got confused and slightly uncomfortable, so I connected with my Akashic records and asked for the masters' presence and advice. They reminded me that Mother Earth is everywhere and that I need to learn to accept love, no matter where it comes from and how it comes to me. Love is love—end of story.

Every time I feel I am losing myself, I connect to the Akashic records and get quickly and lovingly reminded of who I am and what my true self and essence are. This is a gift I am eternally grateful for having received in this life.

How Can People Connect to the Akashic Records?

Maybe by now you are eager to learn how to connect with your own Akashic records, or at least you are curious to hear what a channeler who can connect to the records has to say to you. But how can a person connect to the records in the first place? Are a bat's claw, wolverine blood, and a bunch of herbs collected at moonlight required for this? No, not at all. It is actually quite easy.

Connecting to the Akashic records is easy. All you need to do is synchronize your energy level with the energy level of the records in order for the connection to happen (kind of like finding the frequency of a radio station). But here comes the tricky part. To resonate on the same frequency as the records means to resonate on the frequency of unconditional love. In the past, this was almost impossible for a human being to achieve; we were more of the vindictive "eye for an eye, tooth for a tooth" kind of creatures. But as centuries passed, we grew more into our understanding of good and evil and started choosing the side of love more often. In the past, it was a no-brainer that if your neighbor stole your goat, you went and cut his hand. Nowadays, even the thought of consciously hurting someone makes most of us cringe. That is why connecting to the records nowadays is very much possible and can be achieved with much more ease by many people.

It touched my heart when I saw a news story on TV once about the mother of a teenage boy who was killed by some drug-addicted teenage gang. His mother was at the murder trial of the young man who pulled the trigger. The parents of the murderer had disowned him after what happened and were not present in the courtroom. The mother of the dead boy and the boy on trial were hugging each other and crying. The mother told everyone in the court room that she loved this young man as her son, because she knew he was not a bad person—just a young child who needed help. She had lost a son and didn't want another young man to suffer and have his life ended. We are definitely not an eye-for-an-eye society anymore.

Now follows the second logical question: "OK, you say that I am ready to open the gates to my Akashic records. But how?"

There are many ways to access the Akashic records, just like there are many ways to talk to God. People meditate, sing mantras, say prayers, perform ceremonies, dance. All are ways to connect with the divine and with the higher realms. However, the easiest and fastest way to access the records, I have found so far, is through the so-called Pathway Prayer.

I considered printing the sacred Pathway Prayer in this book but decided against it. Those of you who already know how to connect to the records do not need the prayer. To those of you who have not established a conscious connection with the records and want to do so, I warmly recommend attending a seminar or reading a book that explicitly focuses on teaching you how to access the Akashic records. Learning how to access the records is not hard; it is your birthright and as natural to you as breathing is. But you need to be properly guided through the process. It is similar to swimming; your body instinctively knows how to swim, and once you learn how to swim, it feels so natural and easy to you, but you do want someone to show it to you the first time, so you can have a pleasant and high-quality learning experience and so that you can swim well in the waters and not just survive without drowning. You can definitely learn swimming on your own, but it is much easier, faster, and of better quality if you have a teacher next to you to guide you and help you along the way. And you also know that you cannot learn to swim like a pro just from reading about swimming; you have to actually try swimming. In a similar way, learning to receive information from the records is a matter of proper schooling and lots of practice; anything less than that would deplete you of using the full potential of this amazing transformational tool and guiding system. For more information on books and seminars that can teach you how to access the Akashic records, you can visit my webpage: https://joyridecoaching.com.

I mentioned the Pathway Prayer. Let me tell you now a little bit more about it. Like every great story, this one has been transferred from mouth to mouth, and in the process, it has become a legend. Here is the story the way it reached me:

A bit more than a hundred years ago, Johny Prochaska was born in Europe into a wealthy family. Procházka is a common Czech surname, but legend has it that Johny's family lived in Spain. Years before Johny was born, a woman took the job of being the nanny of the Prochaska kids. She patiently and lovingly took care of Johny's siblings, until one day he was born; she looked into his eyes and saw that he was the incarnated soul she had been waiting for. The woman knew that a great teacher would be born in the Prochaska family, and her mission was to put him on the path toward his destiny.

From an early age, Johny was different from his other siblings and was rather a loner. An economic crisis hit, and Johny's father was about to go bankrupt. One evening, the nanny, who everybody in the household highly respected because they could feel there was something special and magical about her, sat Johny's father in the kitchen. Shadows from the fire in the fireplace started playing on the walls, and scenes from the future started to appear. Johny's father was to go to Mexico and relaunch his business there. He was to become an even wealthier man there, but he was to know that Johny was not going to be the son he wished him to be and wouldn't be taking over his father's business. Shaken by the information but also full of new hope, the father gathered the family and left for Mexico. Johny wanted to be a good son and tried to help his father in the family business, but the spirit world kept calling Johny strongly. A dream had been following him for many years—a dream of an old woman, sitting in front of an old house, waiting for him with a very special gift.

One day Johny was in Mexico City on business matters and decided to go for a walk. While strolling aimlessly through the city streets, he suddenly saw the old woman from his dream. She saw him too. The moment she saw Johny, she jumped and scolded him: "Where have you been? I have been waiting a long time for you. I have a gift for you. Come back tonight, and I will give it to you." And he did come back later that night. Johny and the old woman started on foot from Mexico City toward the Teotihuacán pyramids, just outside of Mexico City. The Teotihuacán pyramid complex is a stone city, where the great Mayan pyramids of the moon and of the sun are to be found. As the two walked, Johny saw that from all sides. more people were joining them, moving silently toward the pyramids too. Many people came that night to witness and support that which was prophesied to happen.

Johny walked all the way up to the top of the pyramid of the sun, where Mayan priests were waiting for him. The ceremony began. The Akashic records opened, and the lords of the records sent the Pathway Prayer down to earth for Johny to receive. The prayer appeared as a glowing flame scroll above Johny's head, written in the Mayan language, descending into him through his crown chakra. The prayer was not given to him on a written piece of paper; it was engraved in his heart and soul. Johny was given the sacred words, the keys to the Akashic records, the Pathway Prayer. From this moment onward, it became his life's mission to spread the knowledge and teach the prayer to the people of the earth. It was the beginning of a great awakening for the human race.

Johny moved to the USA. He translated the Pathway Prayer from Mayan to Spanish and English and started teaching people in the USA how to connect to the Akashic records. He taught many the prayer but schooled only one to teach it too. This student was Mary Dean Parker. Mary continued Johny's mission after his death (his grave is unknown; he simply disappeared one day). She taught the prayer to many more people and schooled many teachers to spread the word. The prayer is by now translated into many languages. Books were written, classes were taught, the word about the Akashic records spread like wildfire, and now it has reached you too. You and I are Johny's legacy. The lords of the Akashic records are cheering for us to be the light this world needs, to be the messengers of the most important message—the message of peace, joy, and unconditional love.

CHAPTER 2

Life Lessons from the Records

You are not the victim of the world, but rather the master of your own
destiny. It is your choices and decisions that determine your destiny.
—*Roy T. Bennett*

Where it flows in your life, you give freely; where it does not flow,
you want to take. Have you noticed this? When you feel you have
a lot of money, you are relaxed and feel generous. When you are in
love, you want to help people and shower them with attention. When
you are healthy, you are happy to give advice, help, or time to others.
But when you lack something, you expect someone else to give it to
you. Do you think you feel lack because the lack is there? Or do you
think the lack is there because you feel lack?

When you give freely, you live in the flow, and things work
fine for you in that area. While in the areas where things are not
working well for you, you are in a state of lack and wanting to
receive from the outside. The faulty thinking here is that if you
need something, you look for it outside of you and expect others
to give it to you. If you need money, you hope some rich aunt will
leave you a big inheritance. If you need health, you hope someone

else will tell you what to do, so you can restore your health. If you need love, you look for a romantic partner to give you love, or you get a child, who you think is obliged to always love and respect you. With this kind of thinking, you are working in dissonance with the laws of the universe; you are in effect creating your own misery. You cannot be successful this way. Trust the evidence you are seeing in your own life. Needing perpetuates your lack, and giving multiplies your rewards, not vice versa. If you need love, give love; if you need money, give to those who need it more than you; if you need health, help others get healthy. Does it sound illogical to you? Where has your logic brought you so far? Let me show you a different approach.

In this chapter, we are going to connect the divine and the earthly. In Bulgaria, the country I was born in, we have a saying, "A hungry bear does not dance." What does this mean? It means that it is very difficult to dedicate yourself to the higher purposes of your soul when your human earthly needs are not met. It is not impossible, but it is not easy, and it is not necessary. We did not come on earth to suffer. We did not come here to reject the material world. On the contrary! We came here so we can become masters of the divine and of the earthly. That is why I believe it is highly important to learn to deal with our earthly life problems. When our basic human needs are met, we will become much more receptive to the divine paths that have been laid in front of us.

So, let us delve into the messy, beautiful, magical, rewarding, and emotional part of being a human being here on earth and explore what advice the masters have for us. Are you ready for the next chapter of your life to begin? Let's do this!

Lesson 1:
Your Relationships

Throughout life, we all meet different people—nice people and not so nice ones; some we immediately fall in love with and some we need time to warm up to; people who help us and people who hurt us; an entire menagerie of souls who cross our earthly path. However, it is important to know that *no* longer-lasting encounter is accidental! There is a reason you met a person, and finding this reason is the key to healing most of your relationships. Do you want to know what this reason is? Keep on reading.

Meet Karma

Most of us have had many, many lifetimes before we reincarnated into this one. For good or for worse, it is sometimes hard for people to let go of what happened in the past, so they take the experience over into the next lifetime. Maybe a wife loved her husband so much that she was not ready to let him go when he died, and in her next lifetime, she is looking and waiting for him and is thus unable to enter a romantic relationship with another man. Such women crave love, but no man is good enough. Or maybe a man was a monk in a past life and gave an oath of silence, and in his current lifetime, he is socially awkward and never knows what to say. Or a baby boy was ripped out of his mother's hands and killed in front of her eyes; when the mother reincarnates again and meets the killer, she may feel a deep hatred for this person, even if this person hasn't been anything but nice to her in the current life. One way or another, many of us experienced a deep emotion in a past life and happened to carry this emotion over to this lifetime. Karma is in essence simply unfinished emotional business. Emotion with determination equals creative energy (notice that I am not saying if it is a "good" or "bad" creative energy).

But why is this a problem? Well, for one, these emotional memories keep us bound to the earthly experience and do not allow us to break the karmic wheel and ascend to higher realms of existence. Also, maybe you are currently suffering because of something that happened in a past life—something that has nothing to do with who you are in this life. One thing is important to understand: karma is never a punishment. If you fall from a tree, you are not punished by gravity, are you? Gravity is neutral and is simply a functioning law. It is our responsibility to respect it. In a similar way, it is our responsibility to respect and live according to the law of karma. All that happens to us now, based on events from past lives, happens because we still have an unresolved emotional charge connected to the events and people of the past. The universal laws are neutral; our life and emotions are in our hands.

The universe is impartial. In the beginning, I thought *impartial* meant that the universe simply did not care, but the more time passed, the more I got convinced that what it actually means is that the universe loves everyone equally, unconditionally, and does not judge. The universe has laws that govern it, and you cannot sway these laws by pleading, cursing, praying, or pretending not to care. And still—no matter what you do, you will be loved unconditionally.

Karma is the universal law of energy balance. Energy does not disappear; it simply shifts and transforms. The rules of karma are pretty simple: the bouncing of the energy ball between you and your karmic partner repeats until one of you decides to drop the ball altogether. You know when any ball game ends, right? Not when one of the teams wins but when the teams just do not pick up the ball anymore (e.g., because the game time is up). This is also how you can discontinue the karmic game—not by having the higher score and winning but by simply discontinuing the game altogether. Unfortunately, for most of us, nobody explained the rules of the karma ball game when we were children. We have been playing the game without understating the rules. Karma is simply a by-product of us not living and also *not dying* consciously.

People say that there is good karma and bad karma. In effect, it is all the same—that which you put out comes back to you. You usually enjoy the "good" karma and want to end the "bad" karma. But the law of karma is trying to simply bring things back into balance; it is trying to bring the stirred universal waters back to stillness. Good karma can quickly turn into bad karma, and vice versa. The way to win at this game is simply to not play it.

When you are in a state of balance and unattachment to earthly affairs, you are able to hear God much more clearly, become one with Him, and merge with Him. And out of this merge with God come all the inspired actions, all the good deeds, and the compassion, but they do not come out of a place of good karma; they come out of a place of balance, fullness, and oneness with God.

So, we clarified that having karma (good or bad) means that you are still attached to someone or something. People talk more often about bad karma, and they mean it as a synonym for punishment. But karma does not equal punishment; karma equals you not giving up— not giving up on the hate ("bad" karmic connection with someone) or not giving up on the love ("good" karmic connection with someone). You reincarnate with a person because you have unfinished business. Simply stated, either you loved each other so much that one lifetime together was not enough for you, or you hated each other so much that you just could not let go at your deathbed of the desire for revenge. Either way, you are not free of this person, and you have, by your own will, entangled your life with theirs. Your goal should not be to turn bad karma into good karma; the goal should be to dissolve all karmic connections and be free to live your life.

Notice that you have at any point in your life the possibility of severing a karmic connection. If you do not do it during your life, you can do it at your deathbed or later, while in the soul realms. It actually does not matter what happened between you and the other person. If you decide to free yourself, you can be free. It is your and only your decision to do so. You do not need the forgiveness or permission of the other person.

Soul Contracts versus Soul Entanglements

I have discussed at length the process of dying and what happens after death in the section "Death of a Loved One." But to put it here in a short form, when you are dying, you have a choice to let go of all of your earthly attachments … or not. If you managed to resolve all karmic relationships in this lifetime, you are ready for a brand-new adventure in the next lifetime. If you have not, you have the chance to take some rest, review what happened, and make a plan for your next life to tackle the problem again, hoping that this time you will get it right.

How you die is very important. I don't mean it is important by what means you die but rather in what emotional and spiritual condition you transition from the earthly plane. A soul that gets traumatized at the time of its death might need a lot of time until it heals and is ready to reincarnate again. A soul that dies in rage and does not want to wait for a life analysis with its counsellors can jump straight back into a new life, pushed by its rage. And a soul that has managed to let go of its life and ascend peacefully into the spirit realm is able to review its past life, learn from it, and draw a plan for its next one. This is what happens to most of us.

Usually, after having their life review with their spirit counsellors, souls sit together and decide who wants to play with whom in their next incarnation. The souls take a look at their previous experiences and decide what they would like to do in their next lives. There are more than a couple of things that a soul would like to achieve, so it looks for souls who have similar goals for their next incarnation. Some souls prefer to have a rather loose life plan, while others would like to have a more rigid one, with little space left for diverging. The agreements a soul makes with other souls are the so-called *soul contracts* that will play out during the soul's next life on earth. So you see, there are things that have been planned to happen to you, but they have been planned by you and for you. Your soul has planted milestones in your life to track your progress and to support your development. Of course, nobody likes repeating a class again and again, so the goal is to execute our soul plan as well as possible.

The above is usually what happens when your soul is conscious enough to make decisions about its development and next incarnation. There are, however, many who are not ready to regain consciousness after they cross the death door. They refuse to move their eyes away from the earthly experience and want to return as soon as possible, led by strong emotions—be it emotions of love or of hatred. No angel or counsellor is allowed to dissuade such a soul from jumping into another life (we all have free will), and if the soul wants to go back before it sits at the table, where events are planned and decisions are made, it can do so and continue the reincarnation karmic cycle, without taking a more sober look at its last earthly experience. That is why it is important we work on being more balanced, conscious, and free of our karmic connections, so we are able to incarnate consciously and not blinded by feelings. The strong feelings that drive a soul into its next incarnation are usually connected to another person. These two will feverishly turn the karmic wheel again and again until one of them grows up and ends the cycle. What such souls experience is not a soul contract (because the experience was not planned). They experience a *soul entanglement*.

You can discontinue both soul contracts at any point, as well as soul entanglements. Many of us have both kinds in our lives. Usually a soul contract is made for a reason, and it will be easier to disconnect it once you learn your planned lessons. After resolving the karmic tasks you two had, you can still remain close and at the same time live a happy, free life. See this like a conversation between two grown-ups; you can both sit at a table, talk, and make decisions. When a deal comes to an end, you do not necessarily sever all contacts with your business partner. You might as well just go play tennis together and enjoy life, without talking about business ever again.

On another hand, soul entanglements are a bit messier to resolve, because usually there are a lot of emotions involved. When you resolve the karmic connection with such a person, you usually do not remain together afterward. There was no real underlying friendship there that connected you; it was all pure animalistic emotion (saying this without any intent here for insulting the lovely animals on earth, who are a blessing to us all). When you resolve such a connection, you will feel incredibly light and free. Even if you thought you madly loved this person, you will notice that actually not being together is the best thing that has ever happened to you, because you rediscovered yourself as an individual and are no longer merely an extension of the relationship.

Client Story: The Gang Leader

Here is an example of how souls can incarnate in different roles in different lifetimes, because of unresolved feelings. I performed an Akashic records *past-life regression* with a client (not to be confused with an Akashic records *reading*), putting him into a light hypnotic trance. My client saw himself in a past life where he was part of a small criminal gang in the Middle Ages. The young man had an awesome time drinking with his gang buddies and robbing other drunks of their money. Usually, no blood was spilled, and no big harms were done (from his point of view). In one of the drunk fights, however, the young man was pierced with a knife in the chest and died.

My client was not disappointed from this faith; he was actually quite content with the life he had. When I asked him, however, if he knew anybody from this past life in this life, he said that the gang leader is his father now. The gang leader suffered greatly when the lad died so young and felt highly responsible for it, because he had fatherly feelings toward him. The gang leader was the one who had adopted the young man when he was still a homeless orphan on the streets. The gang leader felt guilty for the young lad's fate. So, in the current lifetime, the soul of the gang leader decided to come back as the father of my client and make sure the young man was well and could live up to his full potential this time around.

My client and his dad did not have a very good relationship. The father wanted to make sure his son had a good career and was making all the right choices in life, which resulted in a lot of power fights and tension between the two. The guilt and the unfinished business were preventing these two people from having a loving and fulfilling father-son relationship.

Breaking the Karmic Cycle

By now, I hope I managed to convince you that it is very much worth it to resolve all your karmic connections as soon as possible. I suppose you are eager to learn how you can actually do it. It is very simple. But simple does not always mean easy.

If you are reading these lines, you are probably on the suffering end of the karmic seesaw, and you want to make the pain go away. The trick to untying a karmic knot is to forgive and forget. If you want to break the karmic cycle, it is important to know that you do not need to make it right per se with this one particular person, who is your karmic counterpart. You are responsible for the way you react and manage your life; your karmic counterpart is responsible for his/hers. So, let go, forgive, and forget. "Holding on to anger is like grasping a hot coal with the intent of harming another; you are the one who ends up getting burned," said Buddha.

Forgiveness is a powerful, powerful thing and often not very easy to do. For a forgiveness cycle to be complete, you need to forgive yourself, to forgive the other person, to forgive God, and then to be ready to let it all go and forget about it. This will untie the knot of the karmic energies for you.

I believe it is clear to everyone that we need to forgive others. But you might wonder why you need to forgive yourself too. We are our most severe critics, so until we manage to forgive our own transgressions, we are not done.

You might be also wondering why you need to forgive God. Well, don't we often get angry at God and scream at the sky, "Why?

Why are you doing this to me/them/the world? Why are you not helping me? Why did you let this thing happen?" We are often very angry at and disappointed in God, and this is something that weighs us down. Our greatest suffering comes from our separation from God and the divine, and we cannot heal this connection if we are upset, angry, and disappointed.

You might ask yourself, "Does it mean that when I achieve forgiveness and resolve the karmic energy between me and my karmic partners, there will instantaneously be unconditional love between us?" Not necessarily. The fact that you decided to grow above the petty grievances does not mean that your karmic counterpart is ready to do so too. And this is fine. We are all free to grow and learn at our own pace. In many cases, severing the karmic connection through forgiveness will soften the heart of the other person too. But in many cases, it will not. There is an intrinsic purpose to the existence of the karmic law in the universe, and it is to teach us to understand God better and to feel what unconditional love means. The person who has severed the karmic connection has come a step closer to this understanding and is free of this particular chapter of the textbook. If the other person has not yet learned their lesson, however, they will find another soul to continue playing the karmic dance with. The freewill decision of your karmic counterpart is not yours to take or influence. You are responsible only for your own life.

Your Family

Some of the most important relationships we have in life are the relationships with our family: the relationships with our parents, children, siblings, and spouses.

One of the most important relationships is the relationship with your parents. It defines to a great extend how you view life. What we learned from our parents plays a huge role in the amount of successes, failures, and challenges we have in life. If you think you didn't learn the best things from them, don't be mad at them. Remember that it was your soul's choice for you to be together.

No matter what your relationship with your parents currently is, you need to bring more love into it—at least for your own sake, if not for theirs. And when you are done healing this relationship, well, there come the relationships with the rest of your family members— spouse, grandparents, aunts, uncles, cousins, brothers and sisters, and of course the best of all—your own children and grandchildren. If you can honestly say that you do not have negative thoughts toward any family member, congratulations. You have graduated this master class of the school of life. Close this book, open your wings, and fly back to heaven … or pick the next life lesson to wrestle with. One lesson down, a few more to go.

During my work as an Akashic records consultant and teacher, I have had many people come to me asking for advice related to a family issue. At the beginning, I was always surprised and saddened by the degree of disharmony and negative feelings in the family—a son who cuts all ties to his parents; a mother who has not heard from her daughter in years and does not want to know where she lives or if she is even still alive; a woman whose mother just died, who cared more about her everlasting fight with her brother and how this will affect the splitting of the family property than sending her mother to the other side with love and dignity. Some of the most intense feelings I have witnessed were related, in a direct or indirect way, to a family member. And where there are strong feelings, there is huge potential for healing and love.

The people, who are closest to you are those with whom you have the most history and who have been with you on this journey called the human experience the longest. They are not random souls. They are your teachers, your guardian angels, and for this, they deserve your eternal love and gratitude. If you knew you had to get hurt in order to learn a difficult lesson, you would assign this task only to your closest, most dear and trusted friend. And this friend, more often than not, comes down to earth with you as a family member.

Client Story: The Blood Debt

Let me illustrate to you with a real-life example the effect of family karma on a person's life. A client, Petra, came to me and asked if there was something she could do about controlling her blood pressure. She explained that her entire family has blood pressure issues. While she managed to keep it under control with medication, exercise, and meditation, recently her blood pressure spiked again. We asked in the Akashic records what else she could do and what the root cause of the condition was.

The masters showed Petra that she and her family have reincarnated together for several lives already. In one of their past lives, they were a wealthy European family and owned a small castle, some land, and the villagers who lived on the land. During these times in Europe, there were many wars, where everyone was fighting against everyone else. Petra's family was no exception, and much blood was spilled because of their whims, egos, and power struggles. Soldiers and villagers were sent to war, to die and suffer, not only because of land disputes but very often simply because one lord got insulted by the drunk words of another. All the pain and suffering brought by the unnecessary spilled blood had to be balanced. It is the honest wish of every soul to restore this balance; nobody is forced by God to do so. We simply know this is the right thing to do, and we choose when and how to do it.

Petra long ago paid her blood debt. She had been working her entire life as a medical practitioner and had helped countless number of people heal. Her career choice was no surprise to me, as very often, souls who are responsible for the death of many people in a past life choose a very humane profession in the next life, in order to balance the karma and also in order to experience the other side of the situation—to view closely the pain of suffering so they never cause it again themselves. Balancing the karma is not only about bringing back the harmony but also about experience. The souls want to experience many different things and grow more into the knowledge of love.

Despite that Petra had already paid out her personal karma, she was still connected to her family and was still participating in the group family karma. The masters explained to her that it was time for her to cut the karmic ties to her family and to disconnect consciously from their joined reincarnations. If they were ready to pay their karmic debt, too, was not for her to force or decide. Only her path was hers to control. Petra was surprised and confirmed that many of her family members were very conservative and unwilling to let go of their personal gain for the good of those less fortunate.

There had been a family event recently that triggered her blood pressure to spike up again, because their political views about society did not match at all. Now that she knew the root cause of her blood pressure issues, she was ready to forgive herself and her family and to let go of the past. This also meant that she was no longer to judge her family members for their actions and opinions. Their path was not hers to decide or condemn. She could still meet with them and love them, of course, but she needed to know that their decisions were not hers anymore.

The masters asked Petra to write on a piece of paper the contract she had with her family. The contract is the family's agreement to reincarnate together, stick together through good and bad, and experience life together. Petra was to put an end date to their blood debt karma and to state that she was officially free from it. Everything that was not a connection of pure love between her and them was to be released. Petra was to forgive her family members and herself for the atrocities they performed in the past, and she was also to ask all the souls they hurt for forgiveness. A karmic cycle was about to come to an end. Her freeing herself was a soul invitation to her family members to resolve their karma as well. The contract was to be burnt at the end. The energy was released.

Petra's blood pressure normalized with time. We sometimes think that a health issue is genetically controlled, while it is not so much our genes that are the same as our family's but rather our karma, our beliefs, and our actions.

All of us have parents. Some of us have children. The parent-child relationship is one that each one of us has to go through and ideally master. There are a few possible scenarios about the reasons for a parent's and child's souls to be born together in a shared life. Let us take a look at the most common ones:

- They have a karmic connection. It could be a good karma or a bad karma situation. Either way, it would serve you both if you make sure to dissolve the accumulated karma between the two of you. Note that if you are in a parent-child constellation now, this does not mean that you were parent-child before. Also remember that severing the old karma between you does not mean in any way that you are severing your actual connection in this lifetime. It only means that you are freeing yourself of the old baggage and are ready to live your life from a clear slate.
- They did not know each other from a past life but met in this one because their soul purposes fit. For example, the mother and the father know each other from a past life; the child knows only the father; they all end up together in one family. In this constellation, the child and the father will usually have some things to work on, and the father and the mother, too, but not the child and the mother. They all have come together because their union will serve them all in their personal soul development.
- The souls of the parent and the child have no personal karma to balance. Either of them or both are highly advanced and awake souls that have decided consciously to reincarnate

together, in order to support each other's mission and better the world. Example: Mother Mary and Jesus.

These are the three main reasons two souls of a parent and a child can come together. We are all connected, but the child-parent relationship is more special. You two have a strong energy flow between you. For example, if one works on him/herself, this can influence the other one. You have some common behavioral patterns, some ancestral karma, similar health conditions, and so on. If one works on these things, the positive results can spill out to the other one. But remember, you resolve the issue for yourself and leave the other soul to decide if it is ready to graduate from the lesson, too, or if it needs more time and wants to continue with the same lesson.

Many parents want to be the perfect parents, and many children want to be the perfect child. There is no such thing as perfect, or at least not in the human sense. In God's eyes, we are all loved and perfect just as we are. We have nothing to fix. We have only accumulated disharmonies to clear, so we are able to recognize divinity when we see it (and divinity is around us all the time). If you are a parent and want to work intensively on yourself, so your child will not inherit from you any negative behavioral patterns or bad family karma, you can absolutely do this, but if your child has chosen to learn a particular lesson in this lifetime, you cannot change this and force a nice life on the child. For example, let us say that the child's soul wants to learn the lesson of self-love through abandonment. If you do not abandon the child, the child will find somebody else to abandon her—a teacher, a lover, a friend, her own child. You cannot save your child from all the bad things in the world, because the soul does not want to be saved. The soul wants to experience that which is necessary to further its development and evolution. This means yes, do work on yourself to be a better parent, and no, do not beat yourself up if you could not save your child from suffering.

Your kids are wise souls who are selecting the perfect time to be born. Every moment is perfect for something. You might have heard about the so-called biological clock—the internal clock that is telling a man or a woman that it is time to have children. In our society, it is more accepted for the women to talk about their deep desire to have children, but men feel this deep desire too. This desire is not only biologically triggered; it is triggered when the right moment comes for the parent's and the child's souls to meet—the moment they have jointly agreed on. You know the excitement when you are about to meet a loved one you have not seen in a long time, and the days before that, you are talking and thinking only about that. It is the same with the desire and excitement to be a parent. The prearranged time has come for the souls to meet, and they can barely wait for it to happen. And yes, this prearranged time is usually in the childbearing age of a person, from a biological point of view, but it has less to do with the animal desire to procreate and much more with the soul's desire to meet a particular soul. If you have the calling to become a parent, do it. It is the moment when both the parents' soul and the kid's soul are ready for the union to happen.

If you have never felt the need or urge to have children, this might be frowned upon by society, but it has nothing to do with continuing some genetic line or not. A person who does not want to have children simply does not need this kind of experience for their soul development. Make sure that this decision is not driven by fear or lack of trust in your abilities but rather from a lack of emotional charge around this topic. If you feel emotional about the topic, you have something to resolve around it; if you are in neutrality, then it is indeed not an experience you need in this lifetime.

There is one specific child-parent connection I would like to mention—abortion. If there was a failed pregnancy or an abortion, it is important for the parents to close all the channels to the other world and to cut the cords between them and the child's soul. (Remember, true love can never be cut; only that which does not serve can). If the connection stays open, it can drain the parents and will not serve them or their future children.

Here are some examples of how such an unresolved connection can negatively influence the mourning parents. The mother might close herself and never want to try to have children again, or she might feel like eating for two for years and gain unexplainable weight. The father might become depressed, because he still feels connected to and responsible for this child but is unable to do anything for her/him. This suffering does not serve anyone. If this is you, forgive what needs to be forgiven, let go of the past, and provide a clean container for a soul to come for the next pregnancy, if this is your desire. And remember, we are our worst judges, not God, not your soul, not the child. They all love you unconditionally, and you should love yourself too.

Your Pets

Let me now touch on a topic near and dear to my heart—animals. Each one of us has a role in this universe, as do the animals and plants. The wild animals usually have a role as a species. For example, elephants can teach us compassion, strength, and beauty, and they also have a specific role as guardians of the planet. Our house pets have the role of supporting us (while we support them too), thus manifesting another relationship in our life that teaches us the next stepping-stone on the path to understanding and living in a continuous state of unconditional love.

Personal Story: My Grandma's Cat

I think I can illustrate the role of our relationships with animals via a short personal story. Here is the story of my grandma and her cat.

One day, years ago, my aunt and uncle brought a baby kitty to my grandparents' house. They had found the kitty lost under a car, and because it seemed to be a stray, starving cat, they took him in. But my uncle and aunt lived in an apartment in the city and could not keep the kitty themselves. Then they had the brilliant idea of bringing the kitty to my grandparents' house. My grandma initially did not want the cat, but she quickly agreed when she saw his cute little face.

Time passed, and the kitty grew bigger and could hop between the neighboring houses. One of our neighbors had many cats, and our kitty started spending more and more time there. There were times when he would not come back home for days. My grandma grew sad. She had fallen in love with the kitty; unfortunately, the kitty seemed to prefer someone else's house.

I decided to check with the masters to see if something could be done. I entered in my own Akashic records and asked to speak with the spirit guides of the kitty. I told the guides of our kitty that my grandma was feeling lonely and loved having him around, speaking to him, and playing with him. I asked the guides of the kitty if it was possible for him to stay with my grandparents and not with the neighbor. They just said, "Will be done," turned around, and left. To be honest, I was surprised that it was so easy—no arguments, no discussions, no explanations. They heard my ask and said it would be honored.

Perplexed, I had to ask the masters what just happened. The answer was simple. Pet animals want to be with and serve people; they need a mission. Our kitty was still young and had not yet chosen a fixed mission/human to care for. By asking, I gave him one. The cat returned to my grandparents' house. Years passed with many happy memories. The cat still went to visit the neighbor's cats, but he always came home in the evening and for his mealtimes. Then one day, my grandmother passed away. The cat remained at my grandfather's side to give him company and continue sharing the love. They both loved my grandmother dearly, and this love and the many years spent together keep them close to each other.

Personal Story: The Dog—The Tenth Family Member

Let me tell you now about a problem I had, a story about a past life of mine and a pet, who the masters did not forget to include in my healing. Our pets are part of the energy milieu we live in and are thus an inseparable part of our life.

As a young woman, I used to live with my parents. When I started with my university universities, I had to relocate to a different city. I moved out of my parents' house and had to live on my own for the first time in my life. Up until that point, I had never felt alone, and (you will see later why I am mentioning this here) I was a pretty neat and well-organized person. When I started living alone, however, my inner sloth emerged. I could not recognize myself, and it is a bit embarrassing to admit, but my apartment was a big mess. I could never invite somebody spontaneously for a visit because they would not have found a place to sit. I tidied only before guests were about to come. I even joked with my friends that they needed to accept my home-cooked dinner invitation so that I had a motivation to tidy and clean my house. So, this was definitely an issue in my life at that time, but I did not consider it one of my bigger issues to tackle, so I never asked in the records about it.

One day, I asked the masters if there was some behavior pattern of mine that originated from a past life. To my surprise, they showed me the pattern of being untidy. They showed me an image of a past life where I was one of the kids in a big, happy family. We were seven kids and were living with our parents and a big, loving, golden-furred dog in a big one-room house. We were very happy together, but of course this one-room house was always a mess—a hot, happy, never-ending mess. It is impossible to keep a house clean with seven small children and a big dog running around. A messy home was a happy home for me. I realized the connection between the past life and my present life. I was living alone, and I was unconsciously trying to bring into my life warmth and the feeling of a family by unconsciously creating the messy, homey, loving environment I remembered from my past life. Needless to say, this was a rather childish solution to my loneliness, but this is how our subconscious works. Thanks to the teachers and masters in the records, this unconscious pattern was made conscious. And the solution? A flowers and water ceremony.

The masters told me that I do not need to hold onto that past life and the love and joy I experienced back then because I am perfectly capable of recreating a loving, loud, happy family in this life as well. If I wanted to combine my happy family from that life with a clean home, I just had to make the decision to let go of the old family and the old pattern and focus on the new ones. They told me that some of my relatives back then are among my acquaintances now, and we are not as far apart as I thought. But this past life was no more, and it was time to redesign my current one.

For the release ceremony, I was asked to take ten roses and throw them one by one from the city bridge into the river, and with every rose to say a few words to that family member (I had received their names too) before letting him/her go. It was something like a water funeral, where watching the roses travel on the river was like honoring the dead and letting go of the past. I was a little bit puzzled why it needed to be ten roses. We were seven children plus my mother and father—nine people. The teachers and masters laughed and said, "Because of the dog—you were ten family members in the house."

Needless to say, after bringing this unconscious pattern into the light of my understanding, and after releasing the energy from the past, it was much easier for me to keep a tidy and clean home. As of now, my past self would have said that my current self is even overdoing it a bit. My house is sparkling clean and always ready to welcome unannounced guests who bring joy and laughter into my life. And I have a dog now, too, who is a very central family member and a constant source of joy and love for all.

Personal Story: The Death of a Loved One

One of the biggest reasons for suffering in our lives is the loss of a loved one. I was debating whether or not I should include deep personal stories in this book, but I believe this story will be interesting to read and can teach us all something. So here we go.

When I was thirty-four years old, my grandmother, the mother of my mother, died at the age of ninety-two. I spent the first five years of my life with my grandparents, because my parents were still students at that time and lived in student dorms, while my grandparents had a big farmhouse. As you can imagine, I grew very attached to my grandparents. They taught me discipline, kindness, love toward the earth, and the value of family. So when my grandma's earthly path came to its end, I was devastated. One of the most important people in my life was gone forever, and I was not ready to let her go … so I followed her in the Akashic records.

The Day of the Death "The Ritual of Current Life Release": My grandmother was ninety-one years old and had been in bed for several months already. We knew her end was near. One day, my mother called me and told me that my grandma had passed away a few hours ago. Even though it was a call I had been expecting for some time, it still ran a shock wave through my system. I jumped on the first plane to travel back home to hug my mom, see my grandma for the last time, and attend the funeral.

It was a two-hour flight, and all I could think of was my grandmother. I entered the Akashic records and asked about her. I had imagined many things, which I could see in the records, but not what followed. I was about to witness the Ritual of Release.

My grandmother was standing in the center of a circle, surrounded by many light beings who were beaming love and light toward her. The masters told me, "Today we welcome back home one of our most beloved sisters." The streams of love and light were like a cleansing shower, melting away layer after layer of heaviness, sorrows, and life burdens. My grandmother was releasing all the heaviness and suffering from the life she had just left … and she looked ecstatic. She did not look like my grandmother anymore. She was now a young woman, around thirty-five years of age, dressed in a white-golden robe, with long black hair, beaming with joy and with a big, blissful smile. She had taken her true, authentic form and was rejoicing at the feeling of finally being free. She was not the one suffering. I was. The angels allowed me to join the circle, not so I could talk to my grandmother or help her but to receive healing for myself and my grief by simply being there. She was standing with her back toward me, and I did not think she knew I was there. I managed to stay only for a little while and beam love and light toward her myself, but my pain from the loss was just too strong, and it was interfering with her cleansing ceremony. She was remembering who she really is; she was remembering her angelic nature and was starting to see life through different eyes again. It was important that I did not remind her too much and too soon of her past life, so she did not decide to stay behind with us as a ghost but rather to continue onward on her path toward the light. In one intense, surprising moment, she turned her head toward me, a luminous smile on her lips, and looked me straight in the eye. I looked back at her and said, "I forgive you," as I know that giving and receiving forgiveness is usually very important for people when they pass away. She kept on looking at me, smiling. I said, "I love you." She smiled even more, turned back, and continued receiving the light streaming toward her. The angels escorted me out of the circle, as I was too emotional to stay in there.

The Ritual of Release is very important. It prepares the soul for its life review. This shower of love helps the soul for what is to come next. Imagine it like a shower you take after a very long and stressful day at work. It helps you relax, leave the worries of the day behind, strip away the past, and reconnect you with who you truly are. The soul cannot look at its life and analyze objectively the things that happened if it is still engaged in the drama of the life. When the soul lets go of the relationships, when all layers are stripped away and what is left is only its true self, then it can look at its life and learn from it, rejoice in it and the collected experiences.

The Ritual of Release can take a long time; it can take days. The masters often say, "We are not in a hurry here. We have time." After the Ritual of Release, the next step for the soul is a conversation between it and a smaller circle of spirit beings and guides. It was not possible for me to watch or participate; it is not for public viewing. If the soul needs a break from the conversation and wants to look down to its relatives, it can do so. This is when you might spontaneously think about the deceased person—the soul looked at you from the heavens and drew your attention. It is like when you can feel that someone is staring at you, you lift your gaze, and they indeed are there, looking at you.

"You can come from time to time, dear child, to check on your grandma," the masters told me. "For now, we will take care of her. We will take care of the heavenly deeds around her death and transition. You take care of the earthly ones. Eleonora is fine. She is home now. We will be looking over you and your loved ones and help you in your grief. The experience opens your hearts and brings you all even closer together. Eleonora will like seeing the love between you flow."

The masters and teachers asked me to handle the funeral with respect, even though I knew that my grandmother was not gone, and I could still connect with her and talk to her through the connection to the Akashic records. They said it was important that when my grandmother looked down at her funeral day, it pleased her that she was honored and treated according to the traditions and that the family was strong and united. They were calling her "Eleonora," which was her official first name (people usually called her "Nora" or "Norka," the shorter version of the name). The masters chose to see her in her full glory, with her full name—the name of a queen, which her father purposefully chose for her.

<u>The Day After:</u> The funeral was on the day after my grandmother left the earthly plane. I again entered the Akashic records and asked about her. This is what the masters and teachers told me: "She is well. She is traveling the world right now to places that meant something to her. With every thought she has, she can go to a different place to visit. She can be one moment with you and the next moment somewhere else. When she is done remembering everything, she can come back and do a life review of the life, having refreshed her memory and having said her goodbyes. Many people have unfinished business—things they have not done, or seen, or said, so now, free from the burdens of the flesh, time, and space, and having a higher perspective on life, she can try to do this. This is why it is good to speak honestly with the deceased—to let go of everything on your chest, so all is said and done and the person is free to go. The deceased might try to communicate with you, but it is mostly to tell you they love you, to give you and to ask you for forgiveness, and get closures."

My grandmother died on the same monthly date on which she was born—the twenty-third. I asked the masters if this is of importance and what it means. They said that if a soul comes and leaves on the same date, it means that it managed to complete all the tasks it had planned for this lifetime. She did a full circle and managed to finish everything on time. I was happy that the hard life my grandmother had was worth it. Her soul had succeeded in fulfilling its plan and could continue now to the next level of its soul evolution. It confirmed to me again the power of love and the strength of the human spirit. My grandmother was born in a poor family that had money to educate only her brother. They used her to work on the farm. She was allowed to go through half of the years of a high school and then graduated from a special school for seamstresses. My grandma's dream was to become a teacher, which she unfortunately never accomplished because she hadn't received the necessary education for this. Her brother got a university degree. But despite all that, my grandmother was never angry at her parents or her brother. She was bitter at life that the family was poor but was never angry at her family.

Later in life, she met other challenges. My grandfather was sent to serve as a general on a battlefield, and nobody knew for months if he was dead or alive. My grandfather has a sword and many medals from the war but never talks about it. It must have been a hell on earth for him. They both loved each other so much. I never heard them fight; they did have their disagreements, of course, but they were usually always resolved within minutes, and no hard feelings were left behind. Many people bittered my grandmother during her life, but at the end, she always remained in a good mood, was forgiving of everyone and everything, and did not harbor any hatred for anyone. She had a tough lesson to learn—one that many of us unfortunately fail—to not allow your love for people to diminish, no matter what they and life throw at you. My grandmother succeeded in completing this one, symbolized by the date of her death. From a numerological point of view, twenty-three (two plus three) equals five, which is an invitation to move into the fifth dimension of soul development—a few steps closer to God and to the understanding of what unconditional love means.

The Second Day After: This was a time of contemplation for me. All planned events had passed. We all had time to sit and absorb what had come to pass.

My family is Christian Eastern Orthodox. At the funeral, everyone had to pour some water and some wine on the grave—such is the tradition. I asked the masters and teachers what the meaning of the water and the wine was. I was trying to sort out the truth and the show in one such religious ceremony. I have noticed that many times people do things just because they are told to, but they do not actually understand what the act means. I was curious. The masters told me that the wine symbolizes the earthly life—the color red of the blood. The alcohol symbolized the illusion, the drug; we are drugged and half-asleep and walking unconsciously through our earthly lives. The water symbolizes the cleansing of the earthly transgressions, a new, clean beginning for the soul, the purity of the heavens, and the awakening of the soul from the delirium of life.

People also bring flowers to a funeral. There are many flowers around the body of the deceased person. The flowers symbolize the beauty of the earthly life and how it withers and dies (like the beautiful flowers that wither and die). It is a lesson in humility and of appreciation of life and beauty while it lasts. A reminder for all of us that our earthly life is tender and does not last as long as we would wish it to, but just as from the seeds of the flowers new flowers are reborn, the soul gets reborn too.

Another thing the people from my region do is to put some of the favorite belongings of the recently deceased in the coffin and on the grave. We did this for my grandmother too. The freshly deceased soul is still very much attached to its earthly life. One of the things very typical for the earthly life is the attachment to the senses (taste, smell, hearing, touch) and the collecting and admiring of belongings. You cannot have an earthly life without at least some attachments. This is the idea of the earth experience for humans—to get attached to the earthly and to recognize later you do not need it because your attachment to God can give you all that you get from your earthly attachments and more. This the soul can realize before or after the death. Putting some favorite things in and next to the grave makes it easier for the soul to let go, because it knows that its things are not lost or forgotten or being used in a dishonest way.

The Third Day After: I entered the Akashic records and asked about my grandmother. I landed in a scene that was so incredibly bright; there was so much light everywhere. The masters said, "It is days of celebrations. One of our sisters woke up from the illusion and came back to us. We will be with her during the mourning and will help and support her in continuing her path. Do not worry. She can never be mad at you for anything; her love for you has been way too strong for this. She is sad for the lost opportunities of love, that a stronger love and connection did not occur between her and some people in her life, but she is content with her life and is not angry, just sad. She knows it has also been her responsibility to kindle that love, and she did all she could at that time, so she is content."

The human being consists of many aspects—the physical body (which in turn consists of material, emotional, and mental aspects), the oversoul (higher self), and the individually manifested soul (part of the oversoul that has decided on this particular earthly manifestation). When the person dies, the body dissolves, and the soul leaves the earthly plane. We, the earth angels, take care of the physical body, and the heaven angels take care of the soul. The soul usually knows what is happening when the body dies and floats away on its own out of the earthly dimension, but sometimes it might not want to leave, or it might not feel worthy of going toward the love it can feel waiting for it. In such cases, the soul gets stuck and remains earthbound until it decides it is indeed time to go.

There are many traditions on earth that teach people about death and prepare them for the moment of transition, so that when a person dies, the soul does not feel confused, unworthy, or bound by overly strong emotions to its earthly life. Once the soul moves on, it is free to come back and check on its loved ones, but the souls rarely go back to the earth itself. They stay in the love and look back at their loved ones and send them their love and support from afar.

All burial ceremonies in all traditions are designed such that they honor the soul and the human body and assist in the transition to make it easier. For example, you can light a candle once a day for the first few days after the death (e.g., the first forty days) to console the soul, to show it that it is loved, and to remind it of the love and light (symbolized by the candlelight) waiting for it in the next stage. Love heals everything. It is the best balm for every sorrow, and it helps everything to follow its natural path. Why are the first forty days important? It is a symbolic time that depicts the transition from the third density into the fourth and beyond. It is also a fixed time given to the soul and to its living loved ones to close all chapters and continue with their lives. In reality, it can take the soul (or its living loved ones) much less or much more time to close all chapters, but it is good to have an official recommended deadline. No soul that has remembered that it is part of God wishes for the living to stop living and spend all their time suffering and wining down because of it. And no human being wishes for the soul of their loved one to get stuck on the earthly plane and not continue the natural path of evolution, healing, and development. Use the time after death intensively to forgive, to close old chapters, and to put your life in order. And then continue onward.

A Prayer to Escort a Newly Deceased Soul

Dear God, may you welcome (Name) back to you with open arms.
Please make her/his transition easy and her/
his awakening into the light grand.
May she/he rejoice among the angels and in your glory.
May she/he never forget how loved she/he is—
down on earth and up in heaven.
May your light always illuminate her/his path.
May she/he always be safe. May she/he be happy.
Thank you. Amen.

On that third day, I entered the Akashic records and asked if my grandma wanted to talk to me. Yes, she wanted to. We talked in the vineyard behind the house; she told me she loves me, loves us all, and asked me to take care of my mother.

A few days later, I woke up because of the strong scent of a famous Bulgarian hand cream "Крем Здраве"—a cream my grandmother loved. I generally cannot smell many things (it is something of a physical glitch I have), but this pleasant scent I felt very strongly, and it even woke me up. When awake, I could still feel the smell of my grandma's hand cream. It was so intensive and so beautiful. I had never experienced something like it before. I knew my grandmother was there next to me. It made me feel loved. I think we both needed to have one last physical meeting.

The Ninth Day After: The ninth day after my grandmother's soul left her body was a Saturday. I entered the Akashic records and asked what the masters had to tell me on that day: "Today you should be kind and should not utter a bad word. The deceased are listening. It is best to not speak at all, or if you speak, let only kind words fall from your mouth, so the dead do not get ashamed from their offspring and be content that they left after them good children. Then the diseased are peaceful. Today is a day for peace—peace for the dead and for the living; do not work too much today, but rather go inside yourselves and forgive what needs to be forgiven and say what needs to be said. That is what the diseased souls want to know—that they left behind love and harmony among their loved ones. There are days dedicated to the deceased ones. Use these days to remember your loved ones and to honor them. That way, you also honor who you are, your lineage, and your future."

A Ceremony of Fire, Flowers, Water, and Earth: When my grandmother died, I was not ready to let her go. Long story short, I was stalking her in the records. I was going in the records every day, a few times a day, and I was following her every step. At some point after finishing asking all my childish questions about "What is happening now? And now? And afterward?" I asked the masters what I could do to facilitate her rebirth in the realm she was in right then. I received a ceremony of fire, flowers, water, and earth.

I was still at my grandparents' house, because I went there for my grandma's funeral. For the ceremony, I was to go in the garden with a small bowl of water, a candle, and some flower blossoms inside. I was to make a circle in the dirt with a big opening (i.e., not a closed circle) and sit in it with the bowl gently lying on the earth. I was to invite my grandma's spirit to join me in the protection circle through the opening, if she was willing to. Regardless of whether or not I felt that my grandma had joined me or not, I was advised to do the following: speak to my grandma as if she were standing in front of me and listening to my words, and for every good or bad memory I was remembering, I was to put a bit of soil into the bowl of water—representing the act of burying the old and letting it get dissolved by gentle love. When I was done, I was to wait and listen if my grandma wanted to tell me something too. I was not to answer—just to listen to her in silence. At the end, I was to pour the contents of the bowl into the soil, while still inside the circle, in order to let go and release the past and my memories of my grandma, which were weighing me and her down. The circle I was supposed to leave as is, in case my grandma needed to stay inside and reflect for some more time.

After the ceremony, I no longer had the need to go into the records and spy on my grandmother. I knew that she was OK and in good hands. We still meet in the records nowadays. I learned a lot from her while she was alive, and I am continuing to learn from her from our conversations in the records. Now I have one more angel in the heavens who wishes me well and sends me love.

Death Is Not to Be Feared

I hope you have realized by now that this one life is not your only life and your only chance of happiness. Unfortunately, many atrocities have been done throughout human history because people are afraid of death. We need to reeducate our society and our children about what death really means. This will save us all so much suffering and confusion.

You can imagine death like going to sleep at night. In effect, at night, our life ends. It takes a pause, and it restarts in the morning. Death is exactly this—the transition from our level of consciousness to another. And so is birth.

People suffer when a loved one leaves the earthly plane because they think they can never be together again. This could not be further from the truth. You can communicate with the soul of the person, your souls can meet after you die, and then your souls can choose to reincarnate together again in another adventure. You will have so many more opportunities to meet.

One of the other big reasons people are afraid of death is pain. We are afraid to die in pain, and we do not want to watch a loved one suffer either. But the time and the way we die is not an accident. Our soul is not so irresponsible as to not plan such an important part of its earthly life. If you yourself are threatened to die in a painful way, this is an invitation to you to transform this or to accept it and to learn a ton of things in the process. If a loved one of yours is threatened by a painful death, there is also a lot you can do and learn while accompanying the person on their path. Make sure that the pain does not make you bitter; otherwise, you risk triggering the karmic wheel to turn.

It is always our decision how we will view a situation in life. As an old Buddhist saying goes, pain is inevitable; suffering is a choice.

How-To Guide for Your Relationships

The people in our lives are one of, if not *the*, most important things in our life. We are not created to live alone on top of a mountain. Most of us came to earth in order to experience a multitude of relationships and to learn through those. Maybe you love people, maybe you hate them, but you definitely cannot live without them. Regardless of the current status of your relationships in general, know that they can be improved (until we reach the state of unconditional love toward one another, there is always one more level to grow into).

In order to improve your relationships, to start new relationships, and to have more authentic relationships, you just need to do one thing—realize we are all one, and as such, there is no reason to fight one another, fear one another, or compete. Once you start seeing God in the other, your human condition has been healed.

Most of us (if not all) have karmic relationships in our lives. These are relationships that we have inherited from a past life, because something remained unresolved within us. It could be that our deep love was abruptly discontinued (e.g., by death), or it could be that one was deeply hurt by the other. One way or another, these are relationships where we still feel attached to a soul. Attachment is not freedom.

How do you know if you have a karmic relationship from a past life with someone? It is usually very easy to feel it. You just need to ask yourself if one of the following is true:

- You have unexplainable positive or negative feelings toward this person.
- Your relationship feels heavy, as if there are thousands of said and unsaid words between you.
- You want to but cannot get rid of the person.
- You want to be united with the person but cannot be.

The reasons for a karmic relationship can be many. But the solution is always only one—forgive, love, let go, and forget.

As we discussed earlier in the chapter, karma is in actuality a single-player game. Once you free yourself of the negative emotions (via asking or giving forgiveness, depending on which side of the fence you are this time), you are out of the game. Whether or not your karmic counterpart is also ready to leave the game is not for you to decide or judge. If they are ready, your act will help them get free too. If they are not ready, they will find another game partner to continue experiencing what they need to experience, in order to learn the ultimate karmic lesson—love.

The masters once gave the example of Jesus Christ. During his lifetime on earth, there were quite a few people who did not like him, who harbored very negative feelings toward him, and who felt deeply insulted by his words and presence to the extent that they wished for his death. Do you think this has influenced Jesus's karma negatively? No, not at all, because he did not reciprocate these feelings. Your life and your emotions are your responsibility. The life choices of others are not.

Giving Forgiveness

The process of forgiveness is oftentimes misunderstood. People think that if they forgive someone, they automatically approve of what happened in the past. Sometimes what happened is something that can never be seen as something that is acceptable (think child rape, for example). In such cases, people say, "How could I forgive such a thing?" The goal of forgiveness is not to judge an event as good or bad. The goal is to release the stuck emotional charge within us and discontinue the repetition of the negative karmic cycle throughout the lifetimes. When you give forgiveness, you do it to free *yourself*. Your forgiveness will set *you* free. It will also give the opportunity to the other soul to get free, too, if it chooses to do so. To forgive is rarely easy to do, but you and your freedom are worth the effort.

Another misconception is that you need to communicate your forgiveness to the other. You don't; it is enough to do it in your heart and to start living your life out of the space of freedom and love. Imagine that the event you want to forgive never existed. What would your opinion of this person be then? Act as if the hurt never happened and shift your reality accordingly. Forgiving someone simply means letting the feelings go; it basically means that you release your wish that the other person gets punished. It means not allowing what happened to have control over your life anymore. Holding a grudge against someone is only hurting you. Remember the Buddhist proverb: "Holding on to anger is like grasping a hot coal with the intent of throwing it at someone else; you are the one who gets burned."

You know that you have managed to forgive someone fully when you can feel only love toward this person and are ready to wish him/her well. Recognizing the illusion of the karmic game and the fact that we are all spirit and sparkles of God's essence is the end of all unconscious karmic reincarnations. Once we have released all our karmic entanglements, we are free to decide if we want to return as a free being to earth or if we prefer to stop reincarnating on earth at all and ascend to other realms and planets.

If you do not know how to forgive, just take a piece of paper and start writing. Write for as long as you need—minutes, hours, days. And when you are ready, send the letter to its recipient, or burn it, or bury it in the ground, or let it fly off a cliff, or let it float on a river. Create your own ritual of letting go. Turn around and start a new life, free of the old and open to the new.

And last but not least, if you know how to work with your own Akashic records, go into the records, call upon the higher self of the person (no matter if the person is still alive or already dead), and have a conversation. I guarantee you it will be a conversation of love, forgiveness, and freedom.

Asking for Forgiveness

The other aspect of karmic relationships is asking for forgiveness. Maybe you are the one in this lifetime who made a transgression toward another. Most of us know how much it hurts to know that you caused pain to someone and that you cannot fix it. Imagine you were distracted in your car and had an accident, hitting a child and putting him in a wheelchair for the rest of his life. Or even worse, your own child was in the car, got injured, and has to be in a wheelchair for the rest of her life. Can you forgive yourself such a thing? Can you ask the child for forgiveness? The problem is that most of us are not convinced we are worthy of forgiveness. Even if we collect enough courage to ask for forgiveness, we are afraid that we will not receive it. However, the universal law is that the moment you are ready to ask for forgiveness, your healing has started.

The one who asks for forgiveness and believes that they deserve it has already freed themselves of the victim-penetrator karmic cycle.

Again, what is important is the letting go—releasing the emotional charge around the situation and the involved people. In God's eyes, we are all innocent and loved. You may communicate your excuse to the other via a candid face-to-face conversation, or a letter, or a phone call, or you can just as well say or write the words without anyone hearing or reading them. If you are given forgiveness by your "victim"—great, you are free; if you are denied forgiveness by the "victim"—great, you are free too. The act of asking for forgiveness frees you; it does not depend on if the forgiveness is given or not. As far as you are convinced that you deserve to be forgiven and as far as you have released the energetic charge around what happened, you are free. God was never angry with you anyway. And if God is not angry, then why should anybody else's anger be more relevant?

To conclude this section, I will remind you—do not forget to ask yourself for forgiveness, too, and to give it to yourself. This is also of paramount importance.

And last but not least, forgive God. Many of us have felt betrayed by God. It was never he who hurt us intentionally, but this does not mean that we do not harbor anger and hurt. Forgive God. This will set you free. You cannot be fully free and happy until you have straightened out your relationship with God.

Maybe you wonder if you should ask God for forgiveness too. God was, is not, and will never be mad at you. God does not need to forgive you. But if you think you have transgressed against God, you need to forgive yourself, because you are the one who is judging you, not God.

Things That Cannot Be Forgiven

Very often, things happen to us that seem unforgivable. When clients hear that they should forgive their abusive husband, or the person who murdered their child, or the relative who stole their inheritance, they cringe and say it is not possible.

Forgiveness is never impossible. To forgive does not mean that you approve of what happened in the past. To forgive means that you free yourself of the old baggage, recognize that you have a soul in front of you and not simply a person, and you are ready to live a life unaffected by the past. You have suffered enough. Put an end to it. To people who think that something is unforgivable, I'd say that by not forgiving, they keep on hurting themselves and their loved ones. In our current life, we are invited to rise within the unconditional love, and to love unconditionally means to love a soul no matter what they have done. If Jesus can do it, so can you. It is just, it is right, and it is doable.

Enjoy the love, be thankful for the pain (for it taught you something valuable), and let go of everything that weighs you down. Remember, a relationship is cleared of all old baggage when in your heart of hearts you feel only deep love for a person and wish him/her well. You would be happy to see the person again, but you are not desperate for this to happen and would also be content if you never met again.

Lesson 2:
Your Romance

A European wanted to make fun of a Native American and asked him: "Why is it that most of your songs are about rain? Is it because you don't have enough rain?"

The Native American replied with a question:
"Why is it that most of your songs are about love?
Is it because you don't have enough love?"

I decided to write a separate section on the topic of romantic relationships, because they are a separate and key part of our lives. It takes courage to look in the mirror and decide that it is time to take your life into your own hands and change what you do not like. Simply complaining about how unfair life is rarely leads to any good results. That is why I deeply respect and bow my head to people who are ready to grow, work on themselves, and find the courage to transform their love lives.

A lady came to me once with a question. She wanted to find a romantic partner and was tired of looking and not meeting anybody fitting. The masters started by explaining to her that she wanted to find a spiritual partner and by doing so was restricting the universe in delivering her a suitable individual. Everyone carries in themselves the spark of the divine; everyone *is* spiritual, as we all are Spirit. The masters even gave her a few examples where a nonspiritual partner could be of a greater benefit to her. They also asked her to not judge people who want to give her love—not to see some love as less important than other love because of the person it is coming from. Love is love. Judging the love being sent your way is an ungratefulness and can only restrict the flow of love that comes to us.

It is similar to someone who is starving but refuses to eat the offered food, because they wish to eat a specific other food. "I see you are starving. Here is a wonderful meal for you." "No, I do not want this! I want a beef steak! Oh, I am so hungry. I am so miserable! Life is so unfair! There is no good food out there. I'm so starving." If we are refusing the goodness that comes to us, it is a signal that we are not that hungry for it and can live without it. Being genuinely grateful for what we have polarizes to us more of that which we are grateful for.

Once my client felt a bit relaxed, the masters took the next thread woven into the situation. She had a father she adored, and unconsciously, it seemed she was looking for a man who was as good as her father. This put another restriction on the universe to deliver the perfect partner. This was an issue that my client was ready to release. She had the chance to cut the energetic cords between her and her father and to stop looking for a replacement for him.

When this layer of resistance to attracting a romantic partner was released, too, the masters moved to the next layer. In a past life, the woman and her father were a couple who was madly in love. They loved each other so much that they gave each other the promise of eternal love. This contract was still at play in their current reincarnation. Part of the goal of a soul reincarnating is for the soul to grow more into its understanding of unconditional love. These two needed to learn that there is not only one soul good enough to be loved by them. Each being is worthy to be loved and restricting the receiver of our love is not an embodiment of unconditional love.

Each one of us wants to love and be loved unconditionally. The field of unconditional love is our homeland, and only there we can finally be our authentic selves. Because of this lesson, the souls of the two lovers chose to reincarnate in this lifetime in a combination that would never allow for a romantic love to occur: father and daughter. They still had the possibility of loving each other and supporting each other, but they were forced to look in a different direction for their romantic partners. This was a great ah-ha moment for my client, as she realized why she had such deep love for her father and why she was looking for a husband just like him. It is hard to compete with the contract of eternal love. The woman had the chance now to break this eternal love contract and to release herself from it, in order to be able to get into a romantic relationship with another man in this incarnation. The masters told her how she could null this contract, which was not serving her or her father anymore. She was to put this contract down on paper, date it, and put an expiration date on it. Afterward, she was to burn the contract and thus destroy it, declaring it null and void.

I found this case to be a beautiful example of how the souls challenge themselves to learn how to love better. There are several pillars to mastering unconditional love, and each soul goes through each one at its own pace and sequence:

- self-love
- love for another being (human, animal, etc.)
- love for all; the realization that we are all one
- merging back with God; returning home and completing the adventure of reincarnation and separation

I believe each one of us understands these types of love on an intellectual level. Feeling them with our whole being is a totally different experience and provides a much deeper understanding. You cannot explain love with words; you have to feel it.

One of the great blessings of working with the Akashic records is the unconditional love I can feel in there. Every time I feel an emptiness of any kind, I can go in the Akashic records and receive a hug or a download of the energy I need in my life at this moment. All I need to do is ask for the quality of love I wish for and open myself to receiving it. This has been one of the most ecstatic experiences in the records for me. If you learn to access the Akashic records yourself, you will never feel alone or unloved ever again. I guarantee you. If you are interested in doing so, just visit my website and explore the recommended courses and books: https://joyridecoaching.com.

Story: Moving into Femininity

A woman came to me to complain that she had recently divorced her third husband and was ready for a new relationship. She wished for the perfect mate. Her complaint was that she was attracting weak men, and this was driving her crazy. She had been thinking for a long time that it was just her generation of men who had forgotten how to be masculine. However, after years of trial and error and examples of successful marriages of her girlfriends, she finally started thinking that the reason for her romantic misfortunes might be in her.

The masters told her that in many past lives, she had been strong men herself and that she is carrying in this life with her the energy of the conqueror, of the man whose word is always heard and listened to and who demands obedience. This was the reason she was attracting men who were softer than her and who were letting her make the decisions in the family. In every union, the system aims toward a balanced state—in this case a balance of masculinity and femininity. In her current life, my client's soul chose to come as a woman, and as a woman, she was bound to be feminine and look for the masculine. So even though she was a very strong and successful woman, she dreamed of being with a strong man in whose hands she could simply melt, let go, and relax. The masters told her that if she wished for a different type of man than the men she had been attracting, she should focus on awakening her femininity and bringing it up to the surface. My client was quite scared that by becoming more feminine, she was going to lose her strength and become dependent on her man—a fear many modern women have. This fear usually comes from lack of understanding of the masculine and feminine energies. None is better or stronger than the other. They each have their strengths, and they each need the other to be in balance.

Masculinity has its way of expressing power and strength, but femininity has power just as well. The masculine energy is quick to react and can produce an enormous amount of energy, which it can invest in a given direction and be very successful. You can imagine the masculine energy like lightning—strong, direct, precise, and wanting and attracting a lot of attention to its achievement. In comparison, the feminine energy is like the wind and water. It takes time to carve its creations (a baby does not pop out in a day or two), but its creations withstand the test of time. Just like the water and the wind carve out shores and mountains, the feminine energy carves life—slowly, steadily, gently but firmly. The feminine energy is a very strong energy—as is the masculine. It simply is a different type of power.

The masters asked my client to perform a ceremony with water and air (remember that the female energy is compared to water). She was to take a big bowl of water and sit comfortably in front of it. Sitting in front of the bowl, she was to simply breathe. When breathing out, she was to breathe out into the water all masculine characteristics that were no longer serving her. When breathing in, she was to breathe in from the water all feminine characteristics that she needed in her life. When she felt that the process was complete, she was to simply throw away the water to release the collected excess energy so that it could dissipate and find a better place to serve.

My client was initially scared of letting go of her masculine strength and firm grip over her life, but this ceremony was gentle enough for her to gain the courage to do it. The masters know us so well. They always find a way to trick us out of our patterns and fears.

How-To Guide for Romance

As with everything else, if you want something and don't have it yet, you first need to shift yourself into the feeling that you have it before it manifests. We've been wrongly made to believe that we need to first see something to believe it. It is exactly the other way around; we need to first believe it and feel it before we see it.

Until we learn how to create our life consciously, we will create unconsciously—that is, our unconscious beliefs will run the show. Your unconscious beliefs and behavior patterns determine how you behave around another person, what you say, how you dress and speak, and what you believe to be important or true. Our beliefs determine our thoughts; our thoughts determine our actions; our actions determine the outcome of our life.

Finding Love

More than with other topics, people tend to believe that there is nothing they can do if they are unable to find a partner. They attribute it to fate, luck, or karma. But your love life is no more karmic than your career, health, or finances. The same laws govern all areas of your life.

It should not be a surprise to anyone that one of the most important topics for people is finding a romantic partner. We are love, and we need love in order to exist and be happy and healthy. That is why when we feel disconnected from love, we are desperate to find it again. It is actually a question of deep-seated need for survival and well-being rather than just a romantic whim.

Have you noticed that for some people it is very easy to find a partner and for others it is very difficult? This is often because it is one of the lessons the person needs to learn. It is also so because of some deep-seated beliefs and misunderstood concepts. Usually those who crave finding a love partner feel disconnected from the ultimate source of love (God) and incorrectly believe that bringing a romantic partner into their life will magically fill in the chasm in their chest. This is the ultimate love each one of us craves—the love of merging with the creator and being engulfed by his unconditional love for eternity. The closest substitute on earth is the love of our children, parents, and romantic partners. So, it is no wonder that we crave each one of these loves in our life, and if we do not have it, we make it a mission to accomplish it. But do we go about it the right way? It is important to understand that if we have difficulties finding love, we usually have some unfinished karma or/and subconscious patterns that prevent us from doing so. The good news is these patterns and karmic lessons can be dissolved. The bad news is it is not always that easy. But it is, of course, so worth doing.

Nowadays, the world is full of people with unmet needs who expect others to fulfill them. We have turned into a society of cannibalism, where we eat off one another's energy, because we do not know how to feed ourselves. We have been taught that sacrifice is great and thinking about our own needs first is egoistic. But is it? How beneficial is it when you leave your needs last? And what happens when you cannot take it anymore? You explode and blame your loved ones for using you all the time (and they usually look at you cluelessly and in awe of what you are talking about). No one else knows exactly what we need; we are the only ones who know exactly what we need, and we should give it to ourselves or ask for it. If each one takes care and provides for his/her own needs, if we give ourselves what we need, the world will be full of satisfied people in harmony with themselves, and heaven will come down to earth once again. Do not expect the other to make you happy; do not look for your happiness in your partner. Learn to fill your bucket yourself, and (only) when it starts overflowing share it with your loved ones. Then we will become not a society of starving cannibals but one of harmony and love.

In the recent years, people have turned their gaze toward their spouses as a love source. In the past, a spouse was a source of financial stability, occasional sexual gratification, and the chance for birthing offspring. Our modern search for a romantic partner is a search for the love and attention that we miss in our life. In the past, people tended to live more connected to their community. The families were bigger, and everyone lived in one big house or in nearby villages. The people met more often at social gatherings and could spend more time with friends and family. With the progress of technology, we could travel farther, afford to live alone, and stay in touch with our loved ones over the phone or the internet, despite a great distance between us. And the farther we went from our birth family, the lonelier our hearts got and the more importance we started putting on our romantic partners. Because this is how it is supposed to go— right? The only person who is supposed to stay with you throughout the biggest part of your life is your spouse. You leave your parents' house, friends come and go, children move out, but your spouse will always be there, providing you with the constant stream of love you so crave. Right? Wrong. The primary goal of our spouses and life partners is not to be the ones who provide love for us; the primary goal of this relationship is to teach us something about ourselves, help us grow, and bring us closer to understanding love. Just like any other relationship in our life, romantic or not.

Before starting on this journey, it should be clear to the adventurer that finding a love partner is not the final destination. The final destination we aim for (even if we do not consciously know it) is merging with the divine creator, with the unconditional love of God. The more you run after human love, the farther it gets from you. Once you stop running franticly around and look within, resolving any karmic and subconscious patterns, once you reconnect with the internal source of unconditional love, the romantic love you dream of will land in your lap. Abundance come to those who have an abundance mindset—be it a financial abundance or a love abundance.

Unconscious Patterns

The unconscious patterns—the programs in your subconscious that are running the show and very often sabotaging you. Here are some examples of limiting beliefs we sometimes have, which influence our relationships:

- "I hate myself. I am a terrible person. I look terrible. I hate this part of my body." (You do not love and accept yourself; it is not fair or realistic to expect others to do it for you.)
- "Men/women always hurt me. Nobody understands me. Nobody cares for me."
  (You are isolating yourself because you are afraid of being hurt and judged.)
- "It is better to be alone. People need a lot of attention and time, which I am not willing to give. People just want to use me."
  (You see people as robbers of your time and resources instead of as helpers who could lighten your burden.)

To identify what limiting beliefs you have, you can, of course, ask in the Akashic records. This will be one of the most straightforward and effective ways to go about it. But there are other ways, too. Take a sheet of paper and start writing limiting beliefs. You can use a writing prompt like: "I do not have a romantic partner because …" and start writing. You can modify the prompt, according to the type of relationship you would like to have. Some of the things you write will ring true, while others will not. Keep on writing. When you think you cannot come up with anything new, leave the paper for some time and then come back and start writing again (your subconscious will have had time to work on the given task and will come up with more ideas). Then read through your list and pick the top three answers that ring the truest to you. These are the beliefs you need to dissolve.

Now to the next step: how to dissolve a negative belief. Here you can be creative. There are so many different methods out there you can use, and many books written on each one of them that can guide you in the process. Here are a few techniques that work great for dissolving a limiting belief: Akashic records consultation, EFT (emotional freedom technique), hypnosis, shamanic ritual, fire ceremony, trance dance, psychotherapy. The world is your oyster.

Often, even making the unconscious belief known to your awake self is enough for you to not live by it anymore. However, make sure you come up with a positive/new belief to replace the old one with. You do not have to do this, but it is better to be deliberate about it instead of letting your subconscious pick one for you. The new belief you choose for yourself should be one that makes you feel free, strong, and inspired.

To sum it up, here is a step-by-step guide for resolving the issues around finding a partner:

1. Take a sheet of paper and start writing all the beliefs you have about love and romantic relationships. Do you feel safe around men, or are you afraid of them? Do you think women just want to use you? What do you think is the role of a spouse? Keep on writing. What do you think about men/women in general? What do you think you can give in a relationship? What do you need from a relationship?
2. Ask a few friends to do the same and then compare your answers. Ask friends who are (more or less) happily married as well as single friends. Do you see the difference in the answers? These are the mind shifts you need to achieve in order to have what others have. Learn from the people who already walked this path successfully.
3. Reverse the faulty beliefs you have. You can use EFT (emotional freedom technique) to shift a negative belief into a positive one. You can use affirmations. You can go to a hypnotherapist to make sure you reprogram your subconscious. There is a multitude of methods you can use for this, but don't get lost in trying to find the best method. Anything you do will bring you better results than not doing anything.
4. Go out there and act. Ask yourself, "What would a person who is great at relationships do now/today?"

Open Yourself to Love

Once you get rid of all that prevents you from having love, you need to open yourself to receiving this love and attention. What does this mean? It means that you should start vibrating on the frequency of love (while before you were vibrating on the frequency of lack of love). Like attracts like. Walk the earth as someone who has plenty of love in your life. Give gratitude daily for all the beautiful relationships and signs of love that are already there. Live this self-fulfilling prophecy. Fake it till you make it. You do not have to wait to see it to believe it; you have to believe it to see it. Be the love. Meditate on love. Give love. Help others find love. Think how a person surrounded by love would act; then be that person.

Love is our natural state; the rest are just old habits.

How to Improve Your Romantic Relationship

Have you noticed that few couples have a truly harmonious relationship? Why is that? Why is it so difficult for people to live in love and harmony with each other all the time? It is mostly because it is not our soul communicating with the soul of our partner, but our pain body is communicating with the pain body of our partner. As a result of this, it is very often our past hurt selves that are having a relationship with each other and not our current selves.

As long as your pain body is driving your relationships, they will always be painful. Healing old wounds will allow you to look at your partner not through the eyes of pain but through the eyes of love. The more past hurts you heal, the more your life will be filled with love—giving it and receiving it with joy, gratitude, and a large smile.

No matter what relationship you find yourself in and how you ended up with this partner, there is zero judgment in the Akashic records for any decision you made in the past. We are always loved, always accepted, and always cared for. The discussions and tips here are meant to guide you toward the highest-potential relationship, which is possible for you; you are, of course, free to settle at any other level of potential you choose. The masters know that one way or another, sooner or later, we will all reach our highest potential and in doing so will go back to our Godlike nature. The universe is timeless, so there is no rush to reach our final destination. But from our human perspective, we want it all right now, and this pushes us toward our evolution.

Here are a few examples of how misunderstandings can occur and how easy it can be to bring harmony back into the relationship:

Complaint: "My husband spends hours watching football and is not spending time with me. He loves his football more than me! How can I make him spend more time with me?"

Comment from the masters: "See every action he makes as an act of love toward you. He spends hours watching football because he wants to show you that it is OK for you, too, to pursue your hobbies or simply have some time off from him. You are two separate individuals who need individual time to return to your core. Remember who you are and refocus on what makes you happy and fulfilled."

Complaint: "My girlfriend is angry all the time and is constantly complaining. What can I do so she is happier more often?"

Comment from the masters: "Can you imagine that she gets angry because she feels helpless at fulfilling your needs? You are putting many requirements toward her, and you want her to change. No one can change because they are asked to do so; the most effective change comes from within. Forcing her into the way you want her to be drives her crazy, and she explodes. Her complaints and anger are actually her loving you and feeling not good enough for you. Ease up on her. Compliment her a lot for the things you like in her. And watch her relax and blossom in front of your eyes."

Complaint: "My partner does not speak with me as much as I would like to. He keeps to himself. I do not feel connected to him anymore. Does he not love me?"

Comment from the masters: "He is afraid that whatever he says is wrong, makes you angry, or is hurting you. He prefers to see you smiling and laughing and not sad and mad at him. When you two are having fun, simply tell him how happy he makes you. He needs to feel relaxed that he will not hurt you, and then he can be more himself around you. He loves you too much, and hurting you is the last thing he wants to do, and currently, the only way he can think of how to do it is simply by not talking much."

People often want to change their partner, as they believe that the issue is with the partner and not within themselves. But they could not be further from the truth. We search and search and search for the perfect partner, and then we find one that we deem good enough and start planning how to change them so good enough turns into perfect. Is this you too? If something triggers you, you are the one who needs to take a look inside and see what the root cause of your reaction is. If you allow another to treat you badly, there is something inside of you that does not believe that you are worthy of being treated with respect. If you have the feeling that you are doing more than your partner, then you are the one who on some level thinks you needs to earn love and attention. If you think your partner does not understand your needs, then you can be pretty sure that you yourself do not understand them fully and are not able to state them clearly. This is not to say that it is all your fault; this is simply to say that your life is in your hands. You can improve your relationship but not through changing your partner—through changing yourself.

Once your actions and reactions change, your partner will change, too, and start acting differently around you. And magically, in front of you appears the partner of your dreams (who was physically there all along). However, remember the possibility that when you grow and change, your partner might choose not to do so, and if you were unhappy before, you might end up being even more unhappy afterward, because the disharmony between the two of you will become even more obvious. However, do not see this as a bad thing but rather as a sign and speeding up of the inevitable. Each one of us has the right to grow toward the love and light in our own speed. You cannot force anyone to change in the same pace as you; we all have free will, and we all will circle back to the creator in our own time. But one thing is clear. If something bothers you, you cannot leave it to fester there. You have to heal this part of you that attracted it into your life. This is one of the main goals of romantic relationships—to hold a mirror in front of you and help you grow.

Many think that the main role of a romantic relationship is to find someone who will love them unconditionally—with all their flawed and beautiful characteristics, someone who will always be there, someone who will finally make their living hell a heaven on earth. Well, if this is what you are looking for in a relationship, you will never find it, at least not in its entirety. A relationship can and should provide you love, security, and wonderful moments, but this is not its primary role. The strong relationships have a common goal (e.g., raising children, implementing an idea, supporting the broader family and community, helping humanity, etc.). A valuable relationship constantly pushes you to grow, to get to know yourself and your partner better, and to constantly become a better version of yourself. The primary goal of a relationship nowadays is to make you evolve. It is not to give you the love you were missing. If you enter a relationship with such needs, you will end up in an interdependent relationship that is not based on unconditional love but on the giving and receiving of a service. As long as you expect your partner to actively do or provide something, you are looking for the wrong thing. The real benefits your partner can provide you are simply their presence and being who they are, because this is what triggers the changes in you. The love you crave you cannot find in a partner; this love you can only find via your connection to the divine. You are looking for the feeling of always being loved no matter what, always being protected, always being supported and cheered, always being cared for, always being appreciated, always having someone next to you, always having someone to rely on, and so on, and so on. You can have all this and more but not from a human—from God. Your partner is your teammate in this journey, not your savior.

Lesson 3:
Your Calling

What is my life purpose? Am I on the right track? Which career option should I choose? Next to the romantic relationship question, the question about career and life purpose is the second most asked question in my coaching practice.

Most of my female clients start with the relationship question and then ask the career question; most of my male clients start with the career question and follow it with the relationship question. In effect, we all want the same: we all crave love and fulfillment. We simply want to be happy. A life without love is an empty life, just as a life that is void of meaning is empty. We all want to create, to make a difference, and to expand our potential.

Every one of us came into this life with a calling. If we follow this calling, chances are we will have a fulfilled and happy life; if we do not, we will feel empty, and things will appear dull and senseless. It does not matter what our soul's plan for us is. It could be to discover a life-saving drug or to nurture children. No one puzzle piece is more important than the other, just as no one life's mission is more important than another. Each one of us is on our path of development, and we each choose the exams we will try to pass in this life. It is not a competition. The only race we are in is with ourselves.

Despite the popular belief, it is very easy to follow our soul's plan, even if we do not consciously remember what that plan is. We just need to do this, which feels good and right. When you go in the direction of what feels good and right to you, you feel happy, you find a meaning in life, and you feel fulfilled. In comparison, when you do what you are told and what you think is logical (but your heart finds it boring or even repulsive), you feel like you are wasting your life and are slowly dying inside. Regardless of what impact your work might have on society. That is why, for example, many doctors heal people but secretly crave to be artists and why many artists paint but secretly crave to save lives. This, which is your life's calling is what feels meaningful to you. It is you who says what is worth for you to dedicate your life to.

The feelings you have around your career are a clear indication if you are following your soul's plan or not. If you are happy, you are on the right track; if you are feeling unhappy, there is something you need to adjust. Of course, if you would like to have these feelings confirmed, you can find the information about your life's calling in your Akashic records. But be prepared to get a surprise. People usually hope that their life's mission is something grand and highly impactful, but these hopes are rather the wish of our big human ego. Our soul yearns to grow and experience new things … not to be the galactic president. Our ego would like to hear that we were born to save the world with our actions; the truth is (and it is actually much grander than what the ego can imagine) we were born to expand God and the universe through our existence. And how do we do that? By learning to love ourselves and others more, by learning to be more authentic and compassionate. After hearing this, many people say, "Oh … I am supposed to learn to love myself and teach others to do the same, by being a living example for them? But this is so difficult! I do not like myself much. Can I just try to invent some kind of a cancer-cure drug instead? The latter sounds so much easier and of service to society!" Our life purpose is never a very easy one for us (otherwise, it would not really be a challenge worth undertaking), but it always brings us a few steps closer to living a heavenly life here on earth. And who would not want that!

Your soul plan consists of the goals, which you wanted to achieve during this life cycle of yours on earth. These goals are rarely things like "buy a red Ferrari" and are more like "learn more about compassion." However, how you will learn about compassion is left to your free will and to the flow of life. The universe is a fluid body and cannot be forced into a certain shape. You can try to jump on the wave, which will lead you to your goal, but how exactly that wave ride will look you cannot predict, due to the fluidity, flexibility, and constant change of the universal body. That is why you are free to achieve your soul's goals in many different material-expression ways on earth.

When you ask the masters and teachers, "What is my soul's purpose?" you will get an answer that your soul's purpose is to be happy, to enjoy and experience life, and to live this life to the fullest. This is your purpose, nothing more and nothing less. If you ask what special steps you should follow to accomplish this purpose, you will be told that the way to do this is to follow your heart, to listen to what brings you joy, and to go for it. Remember that your desires are God's desires and as such are always supported by life.

You are free to change your soul's plan at any time if you so choose. You might achieve your goals early in life, and then you can choose new goals for yourself. You might also take a few lives to achieve your soul goals if you do not feel like working on them so intensely. However, remember that your soul plan was developed in agreement with yourself, your soul partners, your spiritual guides and teachers, and in unison with God's plan for all. You will be happiest in life if you follow the predestined steps. When the universe sends something your way, there is a reason for this. Make the most out of it. The universe (i.e., God) sends things your way so that you can succeed in your endeavors. Nothing is a punishment; everything is a loving help.

Never forget what is important for you, and this is usually not the money, the cars, and the big house but those things that spring a spark in you, things that make you smile, things that open your heart and make it sing.

What Makes My Heart Sing?

The masters often give the advice to do that which makes your heart sing. This is *the* answer to all questions people might have: How do I find my dream partner? How do I make a good career?

How do I stay healthy? Which project will bring me more money? Should I buy this house or that house? The answer is always the same—go for the option that makes you feel lighter, happier, more excited, and more at ease (i.e., the option that makes your heart sing). These emotions are the beacon lights along your way. Quiet your mind, leave your logic behind, and listen with your heart and desires. That is the secret to navigating the river of life—the direction of the most lightness is the direction of the river's flow, and this direction will bring you the fastest and most easily to your desired goal. Logic bases its decisions on the past and its previous experiences, but the future is not the past, and thinking that the future will be like the past is just a guessing game. Your heart and soul are in constant connection with the actual flow of the universe. If something can tell you the future and the will of God, it is your heart.

So, all in all—have fun! Nobody is saying that we need to suffer to learn our lessons. In fact, we are suffering *because* we are not learning our lessons on time. If we pay attention, if we are conscious, if we are not afraid to face our fears, and if we follow our inspirations, then life will be a breeze. God did not create the universe so we can suffer in it. This is an absurd thought. God created the universe like a modelling clay playground, where we all get to play, create, and expand in our potential. So just drop the suffering and go for that which you have always wanted to do. You know what I am talking about—that one thing that never leaves you as a thought, desire, or dream. I am here now to tell you—go for it. And when you go for it, the next door on your path will unlock and open, and then the next one, and the next one. It is a bit like playing a video game. If you do not move forward, you will not unlock the next levels, and no matter how long you contemplate your next move for the next levels, it will not help, because you have no idea what the next levels actually look like. So just play the game and go for your dream. And no, you do not need to quit your day job tomorrow if you do not feel ready for it. The masters and teachers want us all to live in freedom and lightness, financially as well. Be kind to yourself and give yourself the gift of going in the direction of your dream step by step. God loves you unconditionally and will not judge you for not following your heart's calling 100 percent of the time. There is anyway always another lifetime, another reincarnation where you can try again. God is not in a hurry. But maybe you are. Maybe you do not want to repeat the same mistakes and go through the same pain and suffering again. So, do yourself a favor and stop being so calculative and thinking about what others might say or what the economy will be like and simply go for your dream. Go for the lightness. The universe has its way of adjusting itself around you so your dream can happen (remember—your dream is God's dream, for you are him and he is you). And do not give up at the first couple of issues that might come your way. You know what the difference between a master and a student is, right? The master has failed more times than the student has even tried. Become the master of your life; only you can do it. It is worth it.

In my communication with the masters and teachers of the Akashic records, I have noticed more often than not that the right path is quite bluntly laid in front of us. Life is not a struggle. When we do not go against the current, it flows with ease and joy, and the path of ease and joy is laid down visibly for us to choose. What often stops us from taking it are doubts and fears. Yes, we have the right to take another path, just for the fun of it, but afterward, we will have to go back on the right track. Usually the simplest, most obvious answer is the right one. Life does not want to play hide-and-seek with us. It does not want to put riddles in front of us. Life wants the best for us, just like a loving parent wants the best for their children. Below I will share with you a case where the situation appeared to us, humans, as quite complex, and the solution turned out to be … well, more than obvious.

Message from the masters, teachers, and keepers of the Akashic records: "Yes, life's signs are obvious. They are actually not signs; they are a lead for you to follow. Life does not like playing games with you and giving you subtle signs. Life does not want to trick you or make things hard for you. Life follows its natural path, and if you swim against the stream, you will feel it clearly. Here are the signs to look for in you, which will show you that you are swimming upstream: you feel dissatisfied with your life, you feel sad, things are not happening for you, or you have to struggle a lot for things to happen, and when they do, it is not what you were hoping for."

"Here is how life leads you back toward the right path for you: you hear the same advice from many seemingly unrelated people. You see headlines on the TV, in newspaper, in books. You have inspiring dreams that urge you to action. You know deep in your heart what it is you need and want to do. We urge you, dear children, follow the song of your hearts, follow the signs of life, live in the flow of life instead of in a constant fight with it. Life wants the best for you. We want the best for you. Do not be afraid to do what you know you should do. Each and every one of you knows which is the right direction; you might just be afraid to go there. We tell you—there is nothing to be afraid of. We are aware of your hurts, of the pain you are going through, and we tell you there is no pain bigger than the pain of straying away from your calling, from your mission, from your destiny. Please, listen to your hearts, listen to your guides, listen to the call of life. Relax and open up in order to receive what you need to, in order to be able to create what you came here to create and to see manifest what you came here to manifest."

One more note on the topic. It is not so important what you do but *how* you do it. Remember, you were not born to be a teacher, a software engineer, or a carpenter. You have other more general skills and lessons to learn, like for example the lesson of self-love. If you do not feel at peace at your current job, first try to do things differently before trying to do different things. If you haven't learned your lesson, you will have similar difficulties when you take on a new course in life. You cannot escape what you need to learn. Changing your job because you hate it is not a good reason. Change your job because you found something to do that you love more. Do not blame your colleagues or the company for your unhappiness. What human and spiritual lessons can you and have you learned through this experience? Make sure you close a chapter in peace, not in war, for this will be the energy you will take with you into your next chapter. Remember, you are not a victim of life. You are your life's creator.

I would like to share with you an interesting case from my coaching practice. My client, let us call her Rose, has had quite a difficult life. She did not recognize it as difficult though. It looked normal to her and did not trouble her too much. But after yet another crazy story, she reached out to me and asked what the Akashic records could tell her about it. She started explaining her situation to me. It so happened that she had to deal quite often in her life with depressive and suicidal people while working as a bank clerk. She was meeting them everywhere. They were friends of hers, colleagues, and customers. She felt like a magnet for them. She did genuinely care about them and was always helping them as much as she could. However, she wanted to know why. Why her? Why was she the magnet?

This is what the Akashic records told her (translated from German): "You have to realize your own might and power, dear child. We understand why you link power with anger and pain, but we tell you power, used with a big heart, is what the world needs. What was, was. What is, is what matters. The people you meet in your life are mirrors of you; they reflect to you how strong you are. You are being put in hard situations to finally realize how strong and powerful you are. These people simply mirror back to you your own power and strength. Accept it. And then these episodes will cease, as their role will have been accomplished."

I did not know anything about her childhood, but the masters told Rose that the fact that her father was aggressive at home did not mean that strength and strong energy are in general bad. It seemed that she was suppressing her own strength for fear of being like him.

So, life was trying to show her that she was actually a very strong person and that was a very good thing. She had managed to save the lives of several suicidal people, and no weakling can do such a feat! She was to be proud of herself and to recognize her own strength and power.

It was quite shocking to Rose to hear this interpretation and point of view offered by the masters. We usually know that a situation is there to teach us something, and we more often than not wonder what this something we need to learn is. The masters told Rose that what she needs to learn is exactly what the situation requires from her (and is forcing her to display as a quality). And here comes a sidenote. We do not need to learn how to be strong. We already *are* strong. We are a piece of God, and we are one with all. We do not have qualities to develop, as we have them all. We simply need to recognize them in us, to welcome them and embrace them. This is what Rose needed to learn. She needed to learn that she is strong and to accept this and not reject it out of the fear of turning up like her aggressive father. The people in her life were showing her time and time again how strong she was. She saved human lives by happening to be the only one around in the moment of a planned suicide. Life's lessons are obvious; we are the ones making things complicated by overthinking it all. And what did the suicidal people need to learn in this case? The same—that they are strong and do not need to run away from life for the pain to stop. They have the power to turn around their lives for the better.

We often make soul contracts with one another. We want to learn the same thing, and we simply play seemingly opposing roles in the scenario, but in the end, we both learn the same lesson. In the case of Rose and her acquaintances, the lesson was that you are a strong and powerful being, and this power can (and should) be used for good.

How-To Guide for Your Career

Career-oriented people are usually quite busy, and they value their time. If you do not have time to read through this entire chapter, let me give you the gist of it. In every moment of your life, follow your highest passion, without conversing with yourself about what would make more sense to do instead. Just do what you love the most in every moment. This is your soul and intuition speaking to you. Trust it. This is all you need to do in order to be successful. Now go and do it. Be successful. Conquer the world. You like my writing and want to read some more before you continue to your next big success? OK, awesome—keep on reading. I love spending time with you.

The universe is constantly giving you clear signs and directions. When you think about a project, the unexplainable positive emotions that overtake you are signs that you are on the right track regarding your soul's mission, and the energies in the universe are aligned for this action to be successful at that moment. When you get the urge to do something, do it. And do not think you need to focus on one thing and one thing only (i.e., one career, one business, one job). Also, do not think that you need to do one thing for rest of your life. You change, your interests change, the universe changes. The only constant in life is *change*. Even God does not know for sure what the future holds, as he does not know what decisions a soul will make and how quickly a soul will develop.

Feel free to have several sources of income. Switch and adjust your professions as your interests change and stay true to that which makes your soul sing. You want to be happy, right? Then do the things that make you happy. The happiness you feel is a sign that you are on the right track. Trust it and act.

Many people ask me what talents they have. They think they have some great talent they have overlooked. The masters always laugh when they get this question. They say that asking them this question is similar to asking them the question, "What do I want to eat?" Eat whatever you want! You are the hungry one. You decide! Same thing with talents. Do what you like! How do parents check what talents their children have? Do they *ask* them? No, they observe them. A child who is a talented musician loves music and wants to play, sing, or dance. A child who is a talented physicist loves math games and is interested in the planets and the forces of the universe. So, a talent is obviously something you are good at and also something you enjoy doing. There are many things that we are good at. But we do not enjoy doing everything we are good at. So, what is the answer to the question about talents? Do what you enjoy and are good at.

What do parents do to discover some unknown talent of their kids? They test them by sending them to different activities to try out different things. You can and should do the same. If you cannot think of a talent you have, go and experiment, have fun, and find what you enjoy doing and are good at. Isn't this the goal of experiencing life? Would it not be so boring to never have tried grass hockey, or swimming, or drawing, or giving a speech, or dancing, only because someone told you that your talent is X and you should focus only on it?

Talents are natural dispositions we have, and they definitely are good to have. But it is not so important how talented we are in an area as how much time we spend exercising it. Many people have a great ear for music, but there are very few extraordinary pianists. Practice, practice, practice. Only then will you become a master in your field. And how can you guarantee that you will invest and continue investing the hours needed to become a master in something? Your emotions. If you enjoy doing the thing, you will find a way to do it often and long; if you do not enjoy it, you will find excuses. So, we go back to the answer. In order to be successful, just do that which brings you joy, and do it in abundance.

Maybe by now you have built a pretty good picture of what you need to do in order to be successful in your career. Very few souls came to this earth with a predestined career. Most of us came with the desire to build, or to help others heal, or to teach, or to create. But how this desire will manifest in a career is left to our own choice. Someone who has a desire to build could become an architect, a construction worker, or a furniture builder. Someone who has the desire to teach could become a high school teacher, or a university professor, or a homeschooling mom. The choices in front of us are many, and none are carved in stone. As long as we remain true to our calling, we will be happy and successful.

You do not know which career path to choose next? Close your eyes and start imagining how your life could look with your first career choice. Then do the same with each other career choice. Can you feel how some visions are more filled with joy and enthusiasm than others? The one that has the strongest pull and looks most enchanting to you—this is the one for you in this moment. And if you were not able to feel a difference, simply make the images more vivid, expand your vision, and use your imagination. Do not think about which one might bring you the most success; rather, feel which one makes your heart skip a bit from joy. You do not know what the future holds, but your soul knows what it has planned for you, and it will be directing you through your imagination and your feelings toward the choice that is most in alignment with your soul's plan.

It often happens that we know what we want, but life's circumstances do not allow us to have it. If this is the case, do not despair. If a door has been kept shut by the universe, there is a reason for it. Maybe you want to be a freelancer and have a well-paid office job that you cannot afford to let go of. Or maybe you want to be a painter, but you are not finding people to promote you. Or maybe you want to heal people, but the proper education is currently too expensive for you. All of these obstacles are there for your own good; you either need to learn a skill from your current situation before you continue to your desired one (because without this skill, you and your dream will fail), or it is simply not yet the right time for you to make the next step (we live in an interconnected universe of synchronicities). Trust the pull of your soul and do not give up.

Many people give up right before the success is about to happen. Abraham Lincoln lost eight presidential elections before he was elected and became one of the greatest presidents of the United States. Had he given up, the USA would be at a completely different place of development right now. J. K. Rowling's original *Harry Potter* was rejected by twelve publishers before she managed to get it published. During the fight for Indian independence, Mohandas Mahatma Gandhi went on a hunger strike a staggering seventeen times. If you believe in your dream, go for it. Just do not get fooled by the Hollywood movies that success is an easy thing. As Nicklas Lidstrom's coach, Mike Babcock, once said, "Being a good pro is doing the same simple thing, over and over and over again. A lot of really good players are still bored to death with the process, but the really successful ones are those who found a way to enjoy it."

Following your dream takes a lot of work and dedication, but oh boy, it is worth it. Be brave, dear one. Take the next step, and the doors in front of you will start aligning. You do not need to see the future. You just need to know your feelings, have the courage to follow your dream step by step, and not give up until you have reached your final destination. It might take you ten years to achieve your dream, but if you do not start now, these ten years will be pushed even further into your life, or worse—you will simply never experience the desired success in this lifetime. You were not born to be a cog in the machine; you were born to expand yourself and shine your light far into the universe.

Lesson 4:
Your Health

Another topic that is very important to almost every living human being and that comes up quite often during my Akashic records sessions is the topic of heath—our own health and the health of our loved ones.

When someone is sick, people very often hope for a full recovery, but what they usually do not understand is that the healing of a physical ailment can look different for different people. One possibility for healing is, indeed, that the illness gets completely physically removed from the person's life. Another possibility, which is just as valid, is that the physical condition remains, but the spirit gets healed, which means that the person no longer suffers, and the issue no longer negatively influences the life of the person.

You have probably heard of spontaneous remissions or of people having a "terminal illness" but live to a very old age and die from something completely different. A health problem is not much different from any other life problem we might have. Its goal is to teach us something. And just like any other issue in our lives, the problem remains for as long as we have not learned the lesson, and it ceases to exist when we have. Of course, some lessons can take a lifetime to learn or even several lifetimes (these are usually karmic lessons), but every step in the right direction lessens the influence of the illness over our life.

A note to those who might be close to death. Do not despair. Just do your best and let go of the rest. Respect and love your body, respect and love yourself, respect and love your dear ones. Make sure that you forgive as much as you can (yourself, God, and others), come to peace with life, be deeply grateful for the life you had and have, and leave the rest in the hands of God. Remember, death is not at all the end, but it is important how we approach it. Follow the tugs of your intuition and heart, and they will lead you to the right exit point of the situation. Here is a book that I believe is a great lighthouse for everyone—Anita Moorjani's *Dying to be Me: My Journey from Cancer, to Near Death, to True Healing*.

A note to those who might know a person who is close to death. Do not despair. Know that death is just a door and that if your loved one crosses it, you two can still communicate with each other. The people on the other side of the door are even more aware of the love and light, so your connection will be even nicer than before. Forgive and let go, be grateful for the wonderful life you had and have together, give your loved one as much love and support as you can muster, and leave the rest in the hands of God. And do not forget yourself in the process. Your loved one would want you to be happy, healthy, successful, and smiling—now and always. So do it for both of you. Live the best life you can!

The most natural state of our body and mind is radiant health, just like the most natural state of our soul is radiant love. To achieve perfect health, we need to work on all levels of our earthly existence—physical, mental, emotional, and spiritual. Only taking care of the body will not lead to lasting physical health. Only taking care of the spirit will not lead to good health either. The reason for this is that an illness starts getting manifested on the finer energy levels before it gets manifested on the physical level (even illnesses like the flu). The faster we address the root cause of the problem, the faster the health issue will be healed.

Here are a couple of examples of physical illnesses and their root causes. Example one: a person dies in a past life by a stabbing knife wound in the chest and in this life suffers from problems with the lungs. Example two: A person felt helpless and trapped in her current life. She wanted to run away and saw no possible escape. Later she developed cancer. Example three: a person was an observer of some form of violence (in a past or present life) and for one reason or another did nothing to stop it; the energy of the emotional trauma gets stuck in the eyes, so now the person has problems with her eyesight. These are just a few examples about possible physical conditions and their root cause. As you can imagine, in order to heal such a condition, the person needs to address more levels than just the physical one.

Each pain in our lives is there for a reason, but this reason is never a punishment, as some people might think. Even karmic illnesses are no punishment. As we discussed in earlier chapters, karmic energy is simply leftover energy of something we still need to deal with. This is extremely important to understand. We are unconditionally loved by the creator. Unconditionally means that we are loved and not judged, regardless of what we have done. Let me give you another example. Imagine a child gets sick, and the illness cripples him physically for life. The parents also suffer. For an outside observer, this looks like a terrible tragedy. There are, however, so many reasons a scenario like this might occur. It is possible, for example, that one or both parents killed a person in a past life, and the souls were feeling sorry for this and now have decided to take the soul they harmed as their own child and take care of him and love him and pay their debt back. It is not a punishment; it is a decision that has been consciously made; it is a choice. And the soul of the child? Maybe it is a soul that wants to learn to receive unconditional love, and what better way to learn this than through being helpless and in the hands of people who love him endlessly, despite everything he is putting them through. Even if the souls decided to put themselves in this situation because of past-life events or lessons they want to learn, they can at any moment achieve healing and freedom by addressing the root cause and doing the work. And remember, healing means neutralizing the energy. It means lack of suffering and transition into joy, gratitude, and awe (regardless of how the actual physical aspect ends up being).

Now let us look a bit closer at the different aspects of healing.

Healing the Physical Body

Our body strives toward health, but we need to provide it the right environment for this. You cannot deprive your body of healthy food, good water, enough sleep, peace, movement, and clean air to breathe and expect it to function perfectly. That is why when healing a physical ailment, you need to focus your attention on providing as good conditions for healing as possible. Give the body what it needs; it has incredible healing mechanisms.

Meat versus veggies: allow me to make a sidenote about being vegetarian and walking the spiritual path. There are many militant vegetarians, and many that say that eating meat is harmful for the body and soul. Many spiritual people are deemed "not spiritual enough" because they eat meat. A lady came to me once and asked if she should become vegetarian—or was it not necessary? The masters started a dialogue with her by first reminding her that she is a human being and has a material body and needs some kind of food to charge this body with energy or it will die. Animals are living beings that have a soul and feelings and are part of God, but plants are living beings as well and also have a soul and feelings and are part of God. Maybe it is easier for us to recognize the soul of an animal than the soul of a plant (because the animal has eyes, for example), but the soul and the life are there whether we see it or not. So, if you eat animals or only plants, you are still discontinuing the current existence of a living being. In this sense, if you are a vegetarian, do not think too highly of yourself for killing selectively. You are still killing to eat. Having said that, the masters told her that the plant-based diet is of a lighter frequency and is easier for the body to digest and is indeed the better choice for her. However, the goal should not be to not kill (because it is impossible at the current stage of our human existence) or to prove how much better you are than the others (because you decided to follow a more "spiritual" way to feed yourself), but rather the goal should be to merge with the divine one way or another.

Death as such is not a bad thing; the intentions and the way a death happens are what create the trauma and the karma. More key than the mass production and killing of animals for human food is actually the mass killing of people. If we as a species do this to our own kind, how can we expect to be more merciful to the other kinds of God's creations? Everything starts with self-love and self-respect. Killing or destroying any living being is a grave scar for our own soul. We need to find peace and harmony in our hearts, and then we will see it reflected in our world and on our plates. That is why we might experience peaceful meat eaters and militant vegetarians. What you eat should come naturally to you; anything that you force upon yourself is just that—dictatorship by you to you.

Let us discuss the cycle of food and why simply eating vegetarian or vegan does not guarantee you that you are handling yourself and your food with respect. For a food to be pure and nurturing for your body it is important how it is: planted (conceived), grown, plucked ("killed"), transported, cooked, and eaten.

A plant or an animal can be planted on this earth with love, excitement, and blessings—like a loving couple that is creating a beautiful ceremony to consciously conceive a child. Or the plan or animal can be planted with the thought of greed, envy, and profit. What you sow is what you will reap.

It is also important how we take care of the plant or the animal while it is growing. Did someone sing beautiful songs to it? Was it caressed and told loving words? Or has it just been given the bare minimum to survive and been shoved in cramped spaces like the Nazi concentration camps? Remember that every being has consciousness, and this consciousness creates an energetic field around it. If this being was treated badly, all of these sad experiences will become part of it.

How you pluck your food—how you end a life—is of paramount importance too. Has it been done with gratitude and with respect for the life lived? Or was it done on a factory line by people who despise their jobs and with no regard for the miracle of life? Was there a ceremony to commemorate the death, or was it just done in the most unconscious manner possible?

How your food gets transported to you is also important! Imagine a human corpse being thrown around like a piece of meat. How will the soul feel? The actions of the living toward the bodily remains of the soul are important. This is why we are so reverent with everything that happens with the body of a diseased human being. Why do we not act in such a respectful way when we handle the dead bodies of other beings like plants and animals?

How we cook our food is important too. You know that food cooked with love tastes like no other. When we cook our food, we do not simply add ingredients; we infuse it with our energy too— our blessings or our curses toward the food and the people who will eat it.

And last but not least, how we eat our food is also of great importance. Are you eating with awe and gratitude, or are you eating without any thought about what you put in your month and how it reached your plate? In India, people eat often with their hands. This is a great way to put our energy and blessings into the food we put in our body temple. If we utter a word of gratitude and blessing when eating, we will digest the food much better, and our body will extract much more useful substances from the food. Giving thanks, appreciation, and blessings is also a way to undo any karma that might have been created during the process of bringing the food from its origin to our table. Before you start eating, take enough time to bless your food, to thank it for all the sacrifices made. Put yourself in a state of gratitude and awe, and only when you are feeling deep love and connection with yourself and the divine, start eating your food. And pay attention that, while eating, you do not contaminate your food with foul language or thoughts. How you behave while eating is key too. Some people decide to eat in silence, but our minds are capable of speaking, too, so if you cannot keep your mind at bay, do speak but make sure you speak only words of reverence, gratitude, and love.

So, as you can see, how we treat our food during all of the above stages matters greatly. Most people process and eat food unconsciously and thus ingest the energy that has been put in the food during the above stages. Unless you are the one who does all of the above stages, and you made sure to be very present and aware of your thoughts and feelings at all times, your food requires purification before you put it in your mouth. Regardless of what energy has been put in the food before it reaches us, if we infuse it with the energy of love and gratitude, this will trump most of the other lower vibrations that might be in the food. Different cultures have different ways to bless and purify the food. For example, Christians pray before they start to eat. The strongest energy in the universe is love. If you send love and gratitude toward your food, regardless of if you do it via a prayer, a ritual, or another way, all other energies that are in the food will get neutralized.

Value every day of your life and make the most of it. Do not think yourself better because you do not eat meat, or do more sports, or pay a charity that fights world hunger. Do what you do only because in your heart of hearts you believe it to be good, not because you care about what others say is right.

Provide your body with the best food, best water, best sleep and rest, best air, and best movement you can find, and your body and health will be grateful to you forever.

Healing the Emotional Body

Healing our emotional body is of paramount importance. Most of the physical issues we have are due to, or influenced by, an emotional imbalance in us. We are emotional beings, and we feel in every moment of our existence. What does this mean? It means that regardless of what you are doing in any particular moment, there is some emotion in you. If you are busy working, maybe the emotion is joy and excitement or stress and anger. If you are cleaning the house or hanging a picture, you can be in a positive, negative, or neutral emotional state. The underlying emotions we have throughout the day (and night) are the milieu in which our cells bathe. You can live consciously and be as much as possible in a state of joy, happiness, gratitude, love, feeling your connection with the divine. This is the energy soup in which your cells bathe. Alternatively, you can choose to be in a bad mood—angry, sad, insulted, bored—and this will be what your cells bathe in.

Let me explain the above with an example. It is clear for everyone that a child who grows up in an environment of love and joy has a good chance of becoming a balanced and happy individual, while a child who grows up in an environment of violence and fear is likely to have traumas to deal with in their adult life. It is the same for our cells. We are the shepherds of our family of cells, and the environment they exist in is our responsibility. They can either thrive or struggle. What environment would you want to provide for a child? And for your cells? What parent, what shepherd, do you want to be for your body? It is not fair or realistic to expect our cells to be happy and healthy if we ourselves are depressed, angry, and complaining most of the time.

Behind a given emotional state, there is probably an underlying, deeper emotion that originates from an earlier time, like childhood or a past life. This is also one of the goals of psychotherapy—to find the root cause of your current emotional state, understand it, and thus nullify it. When someone insults us, hurts us, or abandons us, we often continue to carry these wounds with us throughout our entire life. There is a popular saying: when you criticize your kids, they do not stop loving you; they stop loving themselves. With time, emotions start accumulating and weighing us down. It even does not need to be something big and traumatic that happened for the emotion to overwhelm you; it just needs to be the final drop.

There are many, many approaches out there for dealing with our emotional traumas. Here I have only one word to share with you—forgiveness. Ideally, an emotional hurt is considered healed when it no longer brings us negative emotions but rather none or even positive ones (e.g., love). For example, your relationship with that one high school teacher who tortured you for years, you may consider it healed only when the memory of past events not only does not trigger negative emotions in you, but you are ready to wish this teacher well and send her your love and blessings. Of course, making the big jump from "You made my life a living hell! I hate you!" to "It was so wonderful to spend this time with you. Thank you for the life lessons. I love you with all my heart and wish you all the best" is definitely not an easy thing to do, but if you persist, you will be victorious and will reap the positive consequences. Forgiveness we do not so much for the others but for ourselves. To forgive does not mean we approve of what happened. To forgive simply means to transform your past, freeing yourself of it, replacing the negative emotions with positive.

I once saw an interview with a person who had combated cancer. I loved his success story; it impressed me deeply. He said that when he heard the cancer diagnosis, he decided to look inside himself for the root cause of his cells losing their orientation, growing angry, and going rogue. He took some months off just for himself and made a list of all the people in his life that had ever, even mildly, hurt him. He made a list of every single individual in his life he could remember that still brought a painful memory. Making the list was a quick task. It took him only a couple of days to complete it. What he did afterward is what took him several months, but he attributed him getting cured from cancer to a great extend to what he did with the people from the list. He forgave them, one after the other. He went through the list as many times as he needed to until he felt that he had let all past grudges go and had only gratitude and love in his heart for these people.

So, here is my invitation to you. Regardless of what your current health state is, make a list of all the people who might have even mildly insulted or hurt you throughout your life … and then forgive them all and let it all go. Choose your favorite forgiveness method to do so. If you are Christian or Muslim, you can pray. If you are Hindu or Buddhist, you can chant and sing mantras. If you are without religion, you can choose another method or ritual that you know. Go through your list and make sure that you touch every single person with your forgiveness, your love, and your blessing. And do not forget to add yourself and God to this list. Sometimes it is easier to forgive others than to forgive yourself.

To forgive yourself is paramount. And to forgive God too. God does not have unresolved emotional issues with you, does not hold grudges against you, and does not need your forgiveness, but you need to bring your affairs with God into peace. Are you angry with God, life, or the universe? Do you blame God for what has happened in your life so far? You cannot be angry with the divine (another human being or yourself) and expect to have a happy, balanced life.

You need to have peace and love in your heart in order to be in harmony. Until you are at peace with everything and everyone, you have more forgiveness work to do. It is not a very easy task but is one of the main ones in your life. So why not take care of it sooner than later? Close the book now, please, and write the first names on your list. You can do it. It is your life. It is worth it.

Healing the Mental Body

Your mental body, your thoughts and memories, can be making you sick or keeping you healthy. A mental hygiene is crucial, and it means making sure you have only thoughts of joy, peace, and love as much as possible.

It is said that our material body changes states the slowest. Then comes our emotional body and its relatively quickly shifts of emotions, and then comes our mental body with the swift switching between thoughts. Do you know what is faster than the speed of light? The thought. Our physical, emotional, and mental states are connected to one another. If we change one, we influence the other ones too. So what do you think is more efficient and fast—to change your body, so you see a change in your emotions and your thoughts, or to change your thoughts, so you see a change in your body and emotions?

Let me give you an example. Imagine a man who is overweight (due to his lifestyle, not a physical health condition). This man feels bad and depressed about himself and thinks that no woman will like him the way he looks. Of course, if he somehow loses the excess weight and builds muscle mass, he will feel better about himself and will have a higher self-esteem (or at least so he thinks). But such a physical change takes time, and usually if our thoughts and feelings are not on board, we lack the drive to continue on the chosen path. So you see, it will be much more efficient if he changes his thoughts and habits, which will more quickly lead him to believe in himself and feel better about himself, which will then lead to better life choices and the inevitable result on the physical plane—a slim body.

You might be asking yourself how you can change your thoughts and though patterns. After all, our thoughts are so slippery, and even when we try to stay focused, our thoughts jump around like untamed stallions. There are many methods out there that can help you gain control over your thoughts and mental patterns. Methods like EFT (emotional freedom technique), hypnosis, and NLP (neurolinguistic programming) can help you exchange one thought pattern with another (e.g., "I am fat, and nobody likes me" with "I have a total control over my life.") But before trying a more complicated approach, maybe you would like to try one that is quite simple and has existed for thousands of years—meditation. With the regular practice of meditation, you can calm the storms in your mind, you can learn to hear your inner voice louder, and you can gain mastery over the constant train of thoughts in your head. Out of the quietness of the mind comes the peace of the heart and the voice of God.

If you do not know how to meditate, spend some time researching it to find the type of meditation that best suits you. There are different types of meditation. You can meditate sitting, lying, standing, or even walking and dancing. The more types of meditation you try, the better you train your mind to remain calm in any situation. My favorite meditations are the still meditations where you simply sit and observe your breath (sounds simple, but it is quite difficult if you have a busy mind), the so-called Metta or loving-kindness meditation (a Buddhist meditation that awakens the feeling of love and compassion in our hearts), and mantra-singing meditations (where you recite a sacred phrase that calms and molds your mind). Do not strive for perfection. Just strive to meditate. Everyone should spend at least five minutes a day meditating. If you do cannot find five free minutes, you should meditate ten minutes.

Healing the Soul

The soul is not sick and does not need healing, but there are some spiritual aspects that we need to consider when we are talking about our health as a whole.

One aspect of the soul healing is the resolution of karmic debts—that is, unfinished business and unsaid forgiveness, related to events from a past life. For our soul to thrive, it needs to be free of past burdens. And do not forget—many physical conditions are actually unresolved energies that are stuck in our system and fester. You can find more details about how to resolve karmic bonds in the previous sections of this book.

Another aspect that contributes to our spiritual health is our connection to our soul's purpose and our soul's to-do list. One of the main reasons for depression is our disconnect with our soul's plan and with God. When life feels meaningless and when it is hard to find a reason to get out of bed, it is usually because the direction you are headed is not in sync with your soul's and God's wishes for you, and you can feel it. We often try to do the right thing that people expect of us, and then our soul bleeds, because it is not what we wish for ourselves. How many people end up in a profession that brings them no joy, just because they studied not that which makes their soul sing but what their parents or society expected of them? How many people marry the wrong person because they went for the safe choice and not the choice of the heart? How many people postpone doing the things they love because they have to do what grown-ups do, and when they retire, they have no more strength or will to fulfill their dreams? It is so sad to see how people waste a life, doing not what they love and crave but something else … something that crushes their soul one day at a time.

If we have lost our connection to our soul and to the divine, we have cut off the source of inspiration and miracles. Our life seems void of meaning, and our body mirrors this. If you feel that life seems to put obstacles in every step of your way, it probably is because it is trying to bring you back on the right track. It is time to go back to the divine; it is time to go back to your deepest soul desires. Many people think that if there are many obstacles in our way, we just have to somehow climb over them. Why? God puts obstacles in your way for a reason. Yes, if in your heart of hearts, you yearn for something, by all means, try and crush every obstacle in your way. It will only make you stronger and teach you what you need to learn for the next stage. But if you walk in a direction that seems pointless to you, and life just becomes harder and harder, this should be a clear sign to you that all these problems are a loving nudge from your soul and from God to change directions.

If you are not sure what your soul wants, this means you have unlearned how to listen to the call of your soul. One simple way to relearn this is to start to listen to your gut for the right thing to do in every moment. What is your deepest desire in this moment? What do you need? What do you want to do? Where do you want to be? Whom do you want to spend this time with? Honor this call and go do what you wish in this moment to do. Honor yourself and your needs, and when you learn to take care of the loudest needs you hear, you will start noticing the finer ones—the needs of your soul and your calling. Everyone came to earth with a plan, and when you do that which you know is right, then you are following this plan, and this will keep you happy, healthy, and fulfilled. When you are tapped into the source energy, there is no force of nature that can prevent you from achieving your goals.

How-To Guide for Your Health

In the previous section, we discussed our health at length. The reasons for an illness could be many, but they mostly fall into the following four categories:

- karmic
- subconscious beliefs
- emotional
- bad lifestyle

Let me give you an example of an illness and its manifestation in each one of these categories. Let us take a stubborn skin condition as an example. A possible karmic cause could be that this person was burned at the stake, and the skin was the first body part that got the shock of pain. If the soul was not ready to forgive and let go of the event, this energy could get transferred to the next lifetime. A possible accompanying subconscious belief could be "It is not safe to show my authentic self (because people will hurt me)," which leads not only to the physical symptoms of the rash but probably also to issues in the career and relationship areas of this person's life. A possible accompanying emotional trauma, related to this illness, could be all the suppressed emotions the person does not dare to express. A possible accompanying bad lifestyle could be a nutritional regime that does not fit this person. We are a complex system, and the reasons for an issue we have are often multiple. If you want to make sure an illness is healed once and for all, you need to address each one of these four categories.

So, how should we proceed with addressing each one of these categories? Let us look into each one of them in more detail.

Releasing old karma. Earlier, we discussed at length the idea of karma and how to release old karmic bonds. It is important to understand that we can form a karmic bond not only with a particular person but also with an animal, country, place, nation, event, and people in general. In Chapter 3, "Readings from the Records," you can find several such examples.

If you would like to know for sure that the reason for an illness is karmic, you should find a way to receive information about your past lives (e.g., via an Akashic records reading, hypnosis session, trance meditation, etc.). But knowing the reason is not a must for the successful resolution of your karma. Regardless of if you know what happened in the past life or not, karma is released via forgiveness and love—forgiveness and love toward others and forgiveness and love toward the self and God. Sometimes you can intuitively sense whom and what you need to forgive (these are usually things and people who get on your nerves; if they do, you are not in love state toward them). You can create your own forgiveness ritual and make the clear statement that you are ready to be free.

Subconscious beliefs. Each one of us has them. Our subconscious has the role of taking care of the mundane tasks of life, while our conscious self is busy with its earthly life. Our subconscious learns patterns and governs our day-to-day life based on them. Such patterns can be, for example, all the techniques you need to drive a car. In the beginning, you need to be very conscious and present when driving, while later in life, driving becomes a habit. The subconscious stores these habits, and this serves us well.

We inherit many habits from our parents and from our environment (friends, teachers, neighbors, countrymen, etc.) that are not necessarily of service to us. Have you ever wondered why a German behaves so "German", or an Italian behaves so "Italian"? While we grow, we pick up many behavior patterns from our environment. The field of environmental genetics is called epigenesis. Many "genetic illnesses" are not really related to our genes but rather to the environment we grew up with. Our parents did it (and they got sick as a result of this lifestyle), and we copied it (which often leads to the same disease). Think diabetes, heart issues, obesity, and so on. Even things like depression can be inherited from our parents in the sense that the way our parents deal with issues and see life is learned and repeated by us.

You may be eager by now to let go of any subconscious patterns that do not serve you. In order to do this, you first need to know what these patterns are, and then you need an appropriate technique to release them. There are many techniques for discovering your unconscious patterns. You can, of course, ask in the Akashic records, but you can also use any other technique that can bring your subconscious beliefs into the light and transform them. Like a bad old habit, it is easiest to replace it with a good one instead of completely deleting it. Here are a few examples of subconscious beliefs and their positive contra-beliefs that could have influence over your health and other areas of your life.

"It is not safe to be me. I am scared to show my real thoughts and emotions. People will not love the real me." This belief can cause many issues, like depression, skin conditions, kidney problems, and so on. We can substitute it with "I am a child of God, and as such, I am created perfect and am needed and appreciated exactly as am I." Can you feel the difference? The first statement makes you cringe and close yourself; the second statement makes you open up, breathe, and expand.

"I am not good enough. I want to disappear. I hate myself." This belief can cause autoimmune diseases, cancer, depression, and so on. It can be substituted with "I am perfect the way I am. I love who I am. I am a beautiful creation of God. I am needed and valuable just the way I am."

"The world is a hostile place. I can only rely on myself. I am all alone." This can cause anger issues, alcoholism, heart disease, and so on. It can be substituted with "We are all one. Each one has his/her own path, but in our essence, we are all love. The world is a safe place to be."

One of the first books that linked unconscious beliefs with physical illnesses was *You Can Heal Your Life* by Louise Hay. The book provides a very extensive list of beliefs and health conditions and is a must-read for everyone who is on the path of self-betterment and healing.

Emotional. It is already common knowledge that if we experience a deep emotional trauma, this could lead to long-term effects on our mental and physical health. Our emotions are tightly connected to our body. The simplest example is stress. Our Western society has already started to understand that excessive stress can lead to multiple health issues. There are many approaches to reducing stress—mindfulness, better time management, learning to say no, and so on. However, the simplest way to deal with our emotions is meditation and detachment from them. Forgive where forgiveness is needed so your past is not pulling you back, and then use meditation to calm your mind and emotions and to cultivate a harmonious state within. When we want to talk to God, we pray; when we want to hear God, we meditate. For more information on the different types of meditation and how to meditate, feel free to check my website, https://joyridecoaching.com.

Bad lifestyle. We know that taking drugs and drinking excessive alcohol is detrimental to our health. But we make lifestyle choices in every moment of the day, and they too might not be the best for our health. Do I sit straight? Do I drink enough water? Do I sleep enough? When do I go to bed? Do I eat sugar? Do I cook at home? How do I spend the hours of my day? Do I consciously try to surround myself with people who make me happy? Do I walk, jog, bike, or drive to work? The answers to these and many similar questions determine our lifestyle. One bad decision will not overturn the cart. But bad decisions and habits that repeat daily accumulate and can lead to chronic issues that medications can control but cannot heal, because as long as we keep making these unwise decisions, we will keep reintroducing the reason for our bad health.

Most of us know what our bad lifestyle choices are. Start from these. Change them first. You do not need to fix everything at once. This could overwhelm you and you might give up entirely. Even a one-degree shift at a time will position you at a totally different location in the future. One of my favorite books on the topic of habits is James Clear's *Atomic Habits*. Change something small in your life that does not feel overwhelming but that will move you in the direction of better life choices. In *Atomic Habits*, there was a wonderful example that stuck for me. It was about how the coach of the French national cyclist team made them world champions. The coach basically took every aspect of the life of his team members and made sure that they improved even by just 1 percent. He asked them to change something in their diet (e.g., swap something unhealthy for something healthier), he asked them to make sure they slept better (change a pillow, air out the room before going to sleep, sleep fifteen minutes longer a night, etc.), and he asked them to add something to their training (stretch more, run five minutes longer, etc.). So, now take a minute and think. How could you change your lifestyle right now for the better, even just 1 percent? Here are some ideas that you might find helpful, but please feel free to add your own as well. Nobody knows you, your needs, and your schedule better than you. Also, please do not overwhelm yourself with too many changes. Be kind to yourself. A slow but steady change is perfect.

- Sleep fifteen minutes longer a day.
- Go to bed fifteen minutes earlier than usual.
- Air out the bedroom before you go to sleep.
- Change your pillow.
- Change your bed sheets to some that are more pleasant to sleep in.
- Buy yourself nice and cozy pajamas.
- Cook a meal from scratch one extra time a week.
- Increase your meditating practice by five minutes.
- Drink tea instead of coffee at least one extra time a day.

- Drink one extra glass of water a day.
- Drink one glass of alcohol less a day/week.
- Put a hair mask on once a month.
- Get a massage once a month.
- Call one (extra) friend a week to chat.

_____

_____

_____

_____

_____

What can you do now to improve your health and life? One step at a time. Step by step, you walk; step by step, you reach your goal.

Lesson 5:
Your Finances

I have many clients who come to me with questions about their finances and future business plans. I see the pain they are in, and I hope that with this chapter, a better understanding about money will spread in the world. We all deserve to live in abundance, ease, and fulfillment.

Regardless of if we like it or not, money is part of our life here on earth, and no matter what people say, most of them would be more than happy to live in financial abundance (except, of course, a few sages across the globe who have moved beyond money and the earthly concerns).

We deserve to be happy; we deserve to feel safe. Currently, most of the issues people have on earth revolve around money and generally around the feeling of lack. The topic of money and abundance in our life is a highly important one, and despite what some might think, it could not be more spiritual. If you are born at a time and place where money is relevant, then the topic is relevant, to a certain extent, for your spiritual evolution too.

A person who is struggling to survive has little time for or interest in spiritual practices. Wars are started because of resources and money. We cocreate this energy of lack in the world, and it is our responsibility to shift it toward abundance and peace. A person who has not mastered the energy of universal abundance has not yet embodied the knowledge that we all live in the field of God's endless love for us. It is time that we change the energy of lack on earth and transform it into the abundance that we are capable of having—for our sake, for the sake of our world, and for the sake of the entire universe. Who we are and what we cocreate with our thought and emotional patterns ripples in every corner of the cosmos. We have a responsibility to achieve abundance in our life.

Let us look the bull straight in the eye. In our society, we have put a stamp on money, declaring it to be some form of evil. Our saints are never rich, and our rich people are depicted like Uncle Scrooge. While a balanced relationship with money is what it takes to live a healthy and abundant life, most of us have unconscious patterns and deep-seated negative emotions around money.

Some people, especially spiritual people, often feel guilty for wanting to have a lot of money. Which saint was a millionaire, after all? Right? One of the reasons for spiritual people to refuse to want more is their belief that by taking for themselves, they take the resources that others might need more than them. So, they decide that money is not that important, and they settle for mediocre living or even poverty. Also, many clients and consumers of spiritual resources expect spiritual work to be cheap or free. How can you put a price tag on divinity? A doctor can charge thousands of dollars for her services, but a spiritual healer is somehow expected to not take money, right? Wrong.

This is all the result of a faulty intake on the subject of money. This view of money is rooted in the belief that there is not enough for everyone to go around. Many believe that money is the root of all evil. It's not. Money is not the root of all evil; human greed and lack of wisdom are. The universe is endless. There is more than enough for everyone to go around. We create our reality. Literally. We are created in God's image, and thus we are creators ourselves. We are capable of creating abundance for ourselves and for everybody else. And besides—poor money being judged in this way—this is not the way to love it unconditionally! You cannot judge something as evil and at the same time claim that you have mastered the art of unconditional love. A person who has truly mastered the topic of money will be able to manifest as much money as she needs at any time. Money is just another form of energy, just another entity in the universe. We need to put an end to our love-hate relationship with money and start to honor and love it unconditionally. Do you cringe at the thought of loving money? Good. Keep on reading.

Many years ago, before there were cars, people saw that the industrialization and the world's population were increasing and decided to analyze and plan the population of horses. Horses were the main method of transportation of humans and goods on land. Horse farms needed to be ready for the constantly increasing demand. Taking into account the growing human population and the advances and needs of the factories, the number of horses necessary for the foreseeable future was unthinkable! Imagine all the huge stalls necessary, the smell from the constant horse poop, all the food for the horses, all the workers needed to tend them. The number of horses necessary to support the ever-expanding humankind was impossible to achieve! Humankind was facing a major crisis! Scientists were panicking! The Industrial Revolution had to stop or at least slow down! And then the car engine got invented.

The universe is endless, and therefore there are enough resources for everyone. If at a current moment it seems that there are no resources, we simply haven't found the next more appropriate resource to use. Same thing happened when people realized that everything in our world was running on petrol ... and petrol is not an endless resource. Panic! Rising oil prices! And then we found out that there are alternative energy sources, like the sun or the water, that are not only better for the environment but are (for all intended purposes) endless. And there are even better and cleaner sources of energy than these. We do not need to live in poverty to make sure there is enough for all. We need, instead, to put our brains and hearts together to find a way to make sure there is more than enough for all. "We can't solve problems by using the same kind of thinking we used when we created them," said Einstein. We need to shift our consciousness into the consciousness of abundance and out of this state to come up with the solutions we need.

In comparison to the spiritual people who think ill of money, there are people who are in love with money and cannot get enough of it. Very often, this is also the result of a nonhealthy relationship with money—the fear of losing it, similar to a wife who is overly jealous of her husband and, out of her love for him, is paralyzed by the fear of losing him. Such a husband-wife relationship is not a fairy-tale marriage. In a similar manner, such love for money, stemming from the fear of losing it, is not of service. When you have a lot of money but imagining you might lose it is terrifying, you dedicate your life to making sure money keeps on flowing in or too much never leaves. This takes a lot of energy and is also not a happy place to be at all.

The truly blessed ones among us are the ones who have learned the laws of the universe and how energy flows. Money, just like any other manifestation, is simply a reflection of our internal state. Money is not the root of all evil or the source of all good; money is a resource in our hands, and what we make with it is our free will and says nothing about money but says everything about us.

There is something we need to clarify. Living in abundance does not necessarily mean having a lot of money. If you have money, great, but if you do not, that is not a problem at all. If you look around, you will find so many examples of people who do not have millions but are living their dream life—traveling the world, providing for themselves and their family, living in beach houses, working just a couple hours a week. And at the same time, you can unfortunately also find many examples of extremely wealthy people who never feel they have enough and who even commit suicide because they lost in a bad deal a few of the many millions they have. Being rich is a state of mind, not a bank statement.

You want to have a car? You realize that you can buy a brand-new BMW, and you will have a car, but you can also buy a secondhand car, and you will have a car. You can even get a car as a gift or an inheritance, and you will have a car. You could also get a brand-new BMW as a company car that technically does not belong to you, but you have a wonderful car to drive just as well. There are so many ways something might come into your life. Do not restrict the universe by expecting a form of abundance to come to you only via an amount of money in your bank account. The universe is a creative partner; allow for its creativity to unfold.

How plentiful we feel has nothing to do with the amount of money we have. It is all in our head, or better said, it is all in our heart and the vibration we emit. Where does the vibration we emit around the topic of money come from? It comes from energetic patterns (e.g., thought patterns, behavioral patterns) we have. And these patterns come from our past. As money is a topic that is present in every family (regardless of how much in detail it had been discussed), we inevitably spent a lot of time soaking in the energetic soup of beliefs our family members have around money. Our beliefs around money can also come from past lives or the influence of an important friend or mentor in our current life. Finding the root cause of your belief or situation can be helpful. The good news is that we can overwrite the old beliefs. The masters of the Akashic records have helped me and many of my clients on our path to uncovering such unconscious energy patterns and shifting them toward the energy of lightness, abundance, and harmony. I convey to every client of mine the message that it is our responsibility to invite the energy of abundance into the world and rid us and the world of the energy of lack.

Money is like love; if you do not think you are worthy of it, it will not come to you. The amount of money we allow ourselves to earn is proportional to how much worth we believe we have. For example, how much we charge our clients for our services depends on how much we believe we provide them with a good service. The amount of money that flows into your bank account has nothing to do with the economy or the amount of resources (e.g., number of potential clients in the region; the search and demand of your service at the moment, etc.). It is important to understand one thing: your energy attracts your circumstances. Remember the example with the horses and the cars? It is not a question of resources. You can blame poverty or many outside factors, but it is in reality an inside job. It is possible that there is an economic crisis, but a person who has never had issues with money will again find a way to be well. And do not forget who causes the economic crises; it is we, again, who create our joint experiences with our joint beliefs.

How-To Guide for Your Finances

There are several common reasons for issues with money:

- The fear of being seen and hurt—fear of opening up and showing your full potential to the world.
- Not believing your own worthiness; lack of self-love and self-respect.
- Karma and past life experiences—for example, experiences with money that brought you pain in the past; oaths of poverty (e.g., being a monk).
- Inheriting unfavorable patterns around money from your environment as a child. Maybe it was your parents' conviction that you have to work a lot to earn an honest living, or your grandmother kept on repeating that all rich people are heartless and egoistic, or your neighbor told you an emotional story that you can get rich only if you break the law.

If you would like to achieve financial freedom, look into each one of these topics and make sure you clear anything that might be in the way of abundance. How can you do this? There are many ways; all roads lead to Rome. The masters of the Akashic records can, of course, help you with that. Alternatively, you can go to a hypnotherapist to access these hidden parts of your subconscious. You can also perform release ceremonies. You can use affirmations. You can journal. You can use acupuncture techniques to free the stagnant energy. You can use vibration and music to do it too. You can use colors and aromas. See which method speaks to you strongly and go for it. How is not important in this case. Instead of looking for the best technique, just start. One door opens another; with every turned stone, you come closer to your goal.

Please free yourself of your limiting believes around money. Please be a channel for abundance on the planet. The freer people live here, the nicer place we are creating for us and for everyone else. People have suffered long enough from lack and poverty. Be the change you want to see in the world. Invite the energy of abundance here. Your growth is our growth. Thank you for your service and your bravery to face your shadows and conquer them.

To conclude this chapter, I would like to share with you a dream I've had since I was a child. I never understood why people need money at all. I was and still am convinced that if each one of us does what we love, we can have everything we need. Imagine you love baking, and you start baking bread, cookies, and cakes. You smile widely, and your heart rejoices when you show and share your creations with people. "Wow, well done! This smells so amazing! You are such an artist! I love your cakes!" Doesn't this warm your heart? People's gratitude and appreciation is your payment. You sharing your gifts with the world is your payment. An artist needs to paint, a musician needs to play, a baker needs to bake, a farmer needs to farm. We each have hobbies, professions, and interests that we do even when no one is watching and no one is paying us to do it. Won't it be wonderful to live in a world where our gifts and talents are what run the economy? And yes, there are people who love cleaning; there are people who love taking care of the elderly and sick; there are people who love farming; there are people who love writing software; there are people who love law and order, and so on. There are people who love doing everything we need to be done. Such a society would of course be possible in a world where greed is absent and kindness prevails. But I believe this is possible to achieve within just one generation. Kids are blank slates. The way we structure our society and educate our young ones defines the world we create and live in.

CHAPTER 3

Readings from the Records

There is no path to happiness: happiness is the path.
—Buddha

Connecting to your own Akashic records is a blessing beyond comparison but connecting to the records of another being is a state of an even deeper awe and reverence. I am forever grateful to those souls who allowed me to peek into their Akashic records and be a channel for the love and the words of the masters. It is a great honor and a great responsibility to be allowed to do so.

In this chapter, I would like to share with you ten stories of clients of mine. They are real stories; however, the names and some details have been modified in order to protect the identity of the persons. I hope you enjoy these stories and learn from them. I believe it is a great chance to speed up our own soul evolution when we learn from the experience of others, so we do not need to repeat the same mistakes and go through similar situations ourselves. This is our gift to one another for our common growth and evolution. Our personal lessons and experiences can serve not only us but everyone.

Until now, the soul evolution on earth was possible primarily through suffering. We suffer, we do not like it, so we try to change and evolve as a result of it. We have, however, already entered a new era of soul evolution—the era of love, where we no longer need to learn through pain, but we can learn via more gentle methods. I am sharing these clients' stories with you so you won't need to go through hardships yourself but can learn these important lessons from the comfort of your reading chair.

The Alien

At the early beginning of my work with the Akashic records, I used to offer short readings at spiritual fairs, so people could get a feeling about the type of information and energy that comes during an Akashic records reading. I did not yet have much experience working with clients, but I had experience working with the records, so I knew to trust the information I received. During one such fair, a woman came to me and said that she had just one short question: "I have always felt like I do not belong. What is wrong with me?" She looked like a totally normal and really lovely lady, and I wondered why she thought there was something wrong with her.

I opened her records and forwarded her question to the masters. "She is an alien," they said.

I gulped. "What do you mean?" I asked them.

"She is an alien soul that incarnated for the first time here on earth. That is why everything looks and feels so weird to her," replied the masters.

I looked the lady in the eye and told her that I would simply repeat what I got from the masters. I have to admit, I felt quite weird repeating the message to her: "You feel out of place here because you are an alien soul that chose to come on earth and this is your first incarnation here, so things still look quite strange to you—our society is different, our values are different, we live in a dense material world, and we are not very nice to each other." I said this and waited for her reaction.

I expected her to look at me with the look of "Here is yet another nuts and fruits person," but instead she said, "I knew it!" She was ecstatic! And so was I. A big smile spread on her face, and she completely transformed. Her beautiful light soul started shimmering and giggling. She had no more questions. She got the confirmation she needed; she was not some weird person who could not fit in. She was a soul from a different planet, and her feelings were more than normal. She thanked me and continued on her way. I think I was more shocked than she was. It was a lovely experience meeting this beautiful alien soul who has chosen to grace the earth with a visit.

Let me now tell you about the Akashic reading I had with another woman who turned out to also be of an alien descent. This time, I did have the full hour to discuss the topic with her, and I was delighted.

When Marie came to me, she immediately started complaining passionately. She complained that people are so annoying to her, a friend of hers annoys her a lot, her neighbors annoy her, and the people who pass her on the street get on her nerves. She gets angry so easily at everything and everyone! She just could not stop feeling angry at people. What was wrong with her?

I listened carefully to Marie's complaints and forwarded her question to the masters: "What is wrong with Marie? Why is she so annoyed and angry with people?" The masters immediately showed me an image of a spaceship, and they started to explain. She has not had many incarnations on earth yet and is still remembering her past lives on other planets. She spent many lives on planets where love was the dominant energy and people were kind to one another. She knows what is possible for the people on earth and for our society, and it is driving her nuts to look at this chaos and how people behave toward one another.

I repeated to Marie the words of the masters. She was quite perplexed. Why would she choose to come to the earth and leave behind her nice life on the more peaceful planets? The masters gave her the following example for her to understand her own situation and motives: A Western-born-and-raised woman goes to another country where women are suppressed and do not have equal rights like the men, but this suppression is seen as something completely normal in this other country, and nobody complains. The people like it the way it is. They are used to their way of life; they even defend it passionately. Now let us imagine that this woman is stuck in this society for a while and has to live according to their ways and views. It would drive her crazy, and she would feel trapped and angry at the people for the way they treat one another and her, and she would not be able to understand why they do not want to change their ways. So, Marie was in a similar way stuck in a society she did not approve of, but she felt incapable of changing. She was just one person, after all, against an entire society.

The masters explained to her that she actually came to earth not to save it or to teach humans a different way of living; there is free will in the universe, and we are not supposed to force our views on another. Marie's soul came into this incarnation on earth to support the current soul evolution and to observe the humans. Her job was to raise humans' consciousness, to collect data, and to get a firsthand experience of human society. She was to learn from humans' mistakes and bring this knowledge to the next place she goes to assist in its evolution. The masters offered Marie a meditation where she can connect to the other worlds she belonged to and bathe in their energies. She could in this way remember who she is and why she came here and consequently relax and have a more pleasurable experience on earth.

These explanations helped Marie to let her guard down, and she started telling me that when she gets angry (when her emotional energy increases), she can actually manipulate electricity and other physical matter. It was not something scary, but it was annoying, and it was one more reason why she did not like getting angry. She said that she had already broken several laptops in this way. Also, her car usually stopped working when she got really angry while driving. The masters explained to her that she has abilities to manipulate matter. They stressed a few times that she should use these abilities for the highest good of all. They explained to her how to harness these powers and how to call them whenever she wants (and not for them to manifest only when she gets angry). They told her to look for a teacher who could teach her further how to work with these powers. Marie already knew a teacher she could go to (as is usually the case; our path is laid down in front of us, and we just need to summon the courage to start walking).

At the end of the session, Marie was feeling very excited and relaxed because she realized she was not weird, and what she secretly knew was true got validated by the masters. She left with a couple of tools to help her connect to the alien worlds she knew so much better, as well as a guidance for how to harness her abilities to manipulate matter at will.

Useful Tip: If you are feeling weird and out of this world, do not despair. It is very much possible that you, too, are an alien soul that incarnated on earth for the first time. Do not make yourself wrong for being different but rejoice in who you are and make the most of your stay here. Nothing in the universe is a mistake. You came here for a reason, even if the only reason was to simply be here. We often are unaware of what a huge difference just our presence can make. As Einstein proved, mass bends time and space. You have mass. Thus, even simply with your existence, you bend time and space. You matter. You are important. You are needed. You are loved. Never forget it.

The Village Beauty

A young man came to me one day and complained that he had very unhealthy teeth and quite a few issues with them. He wanted to know what the root cause of it was and how he could improve the state of his teeth.

We asked the question in the Akashic records, and immediately, the question came back: How is he actually taking care of his teeth? He was embarrassed to admit that he had a poor teeth hygiene. His parents never insisted on him brushing his teeth, and as an adult, despite his sincere efforts, he simply could not force himself to take a good care of his teeth. Of course, bad mouth hygiene can easily lead to multiple teeth issues. The man tried initially to hide this from me, as he was embarrassed, but in the records, everything is stored, and if it is important, the masters face us straight up with the facts. We had now two topics to discuss and resolve: the root cause of his deep aversion to taking care of his teeth and how to resolve it.

The masters explained to my client that he had a past life in the Middle Ages in Europe, in which he was born a beautiful woman. The woman was tall, with long, straight hair and exceptionally beautiful white teeth. Back then, most of the people had terrible teeth, so someone blessed with such good genes was easy to spot. The beautiful woman gained the attention of the local lord, who favored her because of her beautiful teeth, smile, and a slender figure. She received many privileges as a result of his attention, and the people in the village became wrathfully jealous of her. Nobody liked her; nobody wanted to be related to her. She was not the lord's wife, so she was not welcomed in his big house, but she was also not a person of the folk anymore and did not fit in with her fellow villagers either. She had no say in the situation, and she cursed and blamed her beautiful white teeth for everything. If only she had ugly and sick-looking teeth like everybody else! Then the lord would not have noticed her and poured on her all this unwanted attention! Many years passed, and the beautiful woman got older and died bitter and alone, cursing her teeth for the sad life she thought they brought upon her. Needless to say, the desire to have sick and ugly teeth got transferred to the next life, because it carried in itself the hope of happiness and belonging.

My client was quite surprised to hear this, but he felt a relief that his struggle was not simply in his imagination but had a deeper root and meaning. Of course, living in Europe in the twenty-first century, having beautiful and healthy teeth has no negative consequences. Thus, this pattern of cursing and destroying the teeth was of no service to my client anymore. It was time for this pattern to go, if my client was willing to let go of it. And he was. As in most cases, the cure was forgiveness. The masters explained to him that he needed to forgive himself, the village people, and the lord for the inflicted pain. They gave him a forgiveness ceremony, which he was to follow in order to release the old energies.

Once the root cause was removed, it was time to give my client a boost toward better teeth health. The masters gave him some practical advice about improving the condition of his teeth—oil pulling and a special mantra he was to recite while brushing his teeth. The ritual of teeth hygiene was to become a celebration of life and not a sign of destruction and death. The importance a thing has is simply the importance we assign to it.

Useful Tip: Oil pulling is a great way to improve the health of your teeth, gums, and mouth. And just like any other part of our body or an organ, our teeth long for our love and attention. No, it is not weird to speak with love to your teeth. It is a necessity if you want them to grow and stay healthy and happy. Just like children thrive when loved, so do our body and organs.

The Mask

A client of mine, Josephina, came to me and asked about a skin condition she had. It was a weird skin thing, which had been bothering her on and off throughout the years. The skin doctors she went to told her that it was due to a virus, which was all around and was always on the skin and usually does not cause any issues. In her case, however, her skin seemed to be affected by it. She was getting some strange-looking skin patches at random locations on her skin, which were not causing her any discomfort but were nevertheless not normal looking and did not look very pretty. There was also no known medical cure for this condition. The only way to get rid of the patches was with a cream the doctors prescribed, but this was not healing the condition; it was just masking it over while waiting and hoping for her immune system to deal with the problem somehow. The doctors were telling her that the patches would come and go on their own; the only known thing to help so far was exposure to sunlight. My client was living in Germany at this time, where sunbathing was possible only for a couple of months throughout the year. This meant she would have clear skin for a couple of months and fight the condition the rest of the year—and for how long, nobody knew.

I am not a physician, let alone a dermatologist, so when Josephina came to me for a reading, I had to tell her that I would not be able to give her any medical advice. She was curious to know if her rebellious skin was some kind of a divine punishment or bad karma. This I could answer immediately—no. Nothing that happens to us is a divine punishment; we are eternally and unconditionally loved, and what we go through are ways for our souls to learn new lessons and skyrocket on their paths of spiritual evolution. We decided to ask the masters of the Akashic records what they could tell her about the situation.

When we asked in the records about the root cause and the resolution of this issue, the masters confirmed that sunbathing was a wonderful thing for her to do. They also told Josephina that she was to start drinking a lot of water. Drinking water was going to flush away the toxins in her body that were creating the unfriendly environment of her skin. My client was not very happy to hear this. She explained that she was actually drinking on average around half to one liter of water per day—an amount that is way below any healthy recommendation of water intake, but it was very difficult for her to force herself to drink more water. I had to giggle. Usually, our life turns out the way it does because of the decisions we make along the way. A bad decision every day, regardless of how minor, when accumulated over the months and years can have a very big impact on us. It happens very often that the masters give very simple advice that my clients dread following. Why would anyone ask for advice and then dread following it? Because it is not an easy thing for this person to do. If it were an easy thing, they would have been doing it already. And there lies the lesson—through the challenge we grow.

After discussing the topic of water, which took an incredible amount of time to explain to Josephina why and how drinking water is good for her, the masters moved to explaining to her the spiritual root cause of the skin issue. As with many skin conditions, the root cause was an emotional problem Josephina was dealing with. Our skin is tightly connected to our emotions. It is the biggest organ in our body and is the first thing we show to people and the first thing they see of us.

Let us make a short divergence here from Josephina's story and look into the topic of our skin. We all want to look radiant and young, myself included. So, you can imagine that I have asked the masters many questions about youth and the condition of our skin. Here is some of the information I have received throughout the years.

Usually, a problem with dry skin is a symptom of loneliness. We are like a flower that's thirsty for love and attention and starts withering with time. Just like a flower without water starts drying out, our skin starts drying out. The solution here is to allow ourselves to be bathed in the love we so crave. This love is all around us, but we very often judge the sources of this love or simply do not notice them. You could receive love and attention from your family (refer to the section on "Family Relationships" if you experience disharmony on this front); you could receive love and attention from you pets; you could receive love and attention from your neighbors, from your spouse, from your mailman, from your friends, and, last but not least, from yourself. We often wish to get love from one specific source, e.g. a romantic partner, and if we do not get what we hope for, we pout, disregarding all the other love sources in our life.

Another skin condition our world is struggling with is wrinkles when getting old. Have you noticed that some people start looking older sooner than others? And have you noticed that people who work on forgiveness and connecting back with God look young and ageless? There are some quite logical energetic reasons for this. The masters told me once, "The more you heal your heart and release layer after layer of bitterness and old karmic patterns, the closer you come to your true divine image, and it is one of beauty, youth, and health." Isn't this wonderful? By working on ourselves and releasing old patterns, we not only get a lighter, happier life, but we also start looking younger. Someone might say that the speed at which we age is connected to the genes we have. And this is right ... to the extent that our genes come from the same genetic and energy pool as our family. The field of epigenesis has long proved that our genes develop in a way that highly depends on the environment in which the cells and DNA reside. This means that the views and behavior patterns our family has are most probably ours as well, and this means that if we do not work consciously on it, our bodies will develop the same way and age similarly. This is also the reason why many heart conditions and other diseases are deemed hereditary. It is in the genes, but more so, it is in the environment in which the genes develop. Free yourself from your family patterns, and you will free yourself from your family diseases as well.

Now let us go back to Josephina's story. You might be wondering what the underlying emotional cause for her skin condition was. According to the masters, the actual issue was that she had been refusing for years to take off the proverbial mask she was wearing and to show her face to the world. She was a person who was way too unobtrusive to force herself and her opinions on others, thus ending up being tossed around by people and doing what others wanted instead of what she wanted. This submissiveness was something her soul was not ready to accept and was drawing her attention to the truth of who she was. Her skin was rebelling and was telling her that what she was showing to the world was not her true self. It was time for my client to take off the mask, show her real skin, and spread her wings.

As you can imagine, Josephina had no idea how to do this (if she had, she would have done it already long ago). The masters love to prescribe simple but effective solutions. One of the things they suggested was an exercise with a mirror. It is not an easy thing to retrain yourself, change your behavior, and turn from a hiding, shy person into an easygoing, open, and free-spirited one, so baby steps were in order. Josephina was supposed to look at herself in the mirror every day for several weeks and speak to herself words of encouragement, words of truth about how amazing she actually is and how worthy she is of being seen and heard. Josephina needed to start feeling comfortable in her own skin and with her own power, first in the intimate setting of her own company. Once she had mastered seeing in the mirror the magnificent being that she in truth was, she would be ready to bring it out into the world.

Our body has deep love for us. Our subconscious has as a goal to take care of us all the time and at all costs. The wisdom of our soul tries to grab our attention and direct it to an issue we need to deal with, but if we are stubborn, our body and soul will find a way to make us pay attention one way or another. In the best case, we are wise enough to notice the initial signs and address and resolve the underlying issue fast. In the worst case, our stubbornness and inability to listen to spirit can lead to quite unpleasant situations and even death (i.e., a restart of the journey and a new chance to deal with the issue we failed to recognize initially).

Josephina stays in touch with me, and I know that her skin condition disappeared. She lovingly calls it her true-face radar. She heard the message her soul was giving her through her body, and now the soul has a bulletproof way to communicate with her.

Josephina laughs and says that when she starts adjusting herself too much to other people's needs and forgets who she is, the skin patches appear again, sometimes overnight. When this happens, she knows what her body wants to show her, so she takes a moment to readjust herself and reconnect with her true self, and the patches disappear just as quickly as they appeared.

If you have already worked with the Akashic records, you have definitely noticed that they propose solutions that are usually very effective and at the same time very noninvasive and subtle. What a perfect combination! We all wish for a quick, effective, and painless solution. People are usually afraid of change, because they are afraid of the discomfort the change might bring. Because of that, they often choose to remain in a situation, which is definitely uncomfortable but feels familiar. The masters know us very well and always find a way to dampen these fears of ours and lead us very gently toward our healing.

Useful Tip: If you also have the feeling that there is no single person in this world who knows your true self, then you might also be wearing a mask and pretending to be someone else. The masters always remind people: you came here to be you; the universe needs *you*. If you are you, then you will be happy, and the world will be in balance; you will attract people who are a match to your true self, and you will thrive, surrounded by harmonious relationships. God makes no mistakes; creating you exactly the way you are was no mistake.

It is actually more difficult for us to accept who we are than for other people to accept us. Stop being so critical of yourself. Make an effort when you notice yourself criticizing your own actions, appearances, or anything else about you. Stop immediately and substitute that criticism with praise. What did you do right? Make a mental list of that. We don't need to criticize ourselves; life is tough enough. Let's make it easier for once. Love yourself, and don't hide your light. We all need *you* and all of you, just the way you are—perfect.

The masters showed me once a beautiful image that illustrates how we are perfect the way we are, yet we can still grow and expand. It is often difficult for people to understand this concept. "What? I am perfect? But I can still develop. Doesn't this mean that I am not perfect yet?" No, it doesn't mean that. The image the masters showed me was of a beautiful rose bush. The bush is beautiful and full of roses and … simply perfect. Yet the bush can grow and blossom and be just as beautiful. You are this rose bush—beautiful and perfect at every moment of your existence yet with the potential to grow and expand. The client who received this message said that he imagined our planet covered by rose bushes; what a wonderful image—a world where each one of us recognizes our own beauty and not try to twist in order to fit into somebody else's expectations. I say amen to that.

The Old Age, Knocking on the Door

A client of mine, Petra, came to me complaining that she had not slept well in months. In the evenings, Petra was not able to fall asleep. During the night, she was waking up and was walking unconsciously around the house, and in the morning, she could not feel awake for hours. All this was exhausting for her, and she could not wait to hear what information and advice the masters in the Akashic records had for her. To my surprise, however, when I tried to open her records, they didn't open. This happens very rarely, and usually there is a very good reason for this. I got the intuitive idea to create a bubble of protection around myself and my client and then try to open the records again. This time the records opened.

Immediately the masters told Petra that there were multiple reasons for what she was experiencing. One of them was that she was under a psychic attack. There was a woman who was trying to manipulate Petra like a marionette (thus the unconscious sleepwalking where you do something, moved like a puppet by somebody else's hand). Petra confirmed that actually this year she had been visiting a healer who took thousands of dollars from her and whose presence she was constantly feeling in her auric field. The masters explained that the two women know each other from a past life in which they were working together and were practicing black magic. Petra had decided not to do such kind of energy work in this life; the other woman however again got involved in practicing the art of energetically manipulating people.

Once we identified the source of the psychic attacks, the masters showed us what this healer was actually up to behind closed doors. She was afraid she might be left without customers, so when a sick client came to her, she helped him heal only up to a certain extent; she was leaving things unhealed and was even planting new energy imbalances. That way, the client would initially feel better, but later, new symptoms would appear, and because he thought the previous healing session worked, he would come back for another one, and another one, and another one. These actions of the healer were driven by intense survivor fear, which left no room for love and compassion toward her clients. This is actually the way that many "healers" work. It is not difficult to work with energy; what is difficult is to cultivate a pure, loving heart. The ability to work with energy can be used in a serving or harmful way—just like the energy of money can be used to do great good or great evil. A warning from the masters for us all came next: if a person helps you come more into your power, you can trust this person has a good heart and is using an effective healing modality, but if a person makes you feel you need them in order to feel good, run as fast as you can.

Petra was especially vulnerable to the energy attacks of the healer because she had vast chasms in her aura field. Our energy field is like our immune system. If we have a strong immune system, it is very difficult for us to get sick, while a weak immune system can be overwhelmed by the smallest bug. The gaps in Petra's aura were due to several factors. On the one hand, her spirit was ridden with guilt because of the dark magic and pain it inflicted in a past life and was thus convinced it needed to be severely punished. On the other hand, Petra had voluntarily opened herself to the energy of the healer and allowed her in. Similarly to when we go to a physician, if we are feeling bad, we usually let all guards down, trust the knowledge of the physician, and open ourselves up in order to receive the healing we are looking for. I always giggle how a woman, for example, guards fiercely her nakedness but has no issue undressing in front of a doctor. We let our guard down and expose and open ourselves up when we believe we are in front of a person who wants and can help us. And yet no one can break the strength of our free will; if we do not allow someone to enter, they cannot.

The masters led us further. They explained that we needed to first discontinue the energetic connection between Petra and the healer. Then, once the attack channel was closed, we needed to focus on closing the gaps in Petra's energy field so it could protect her against any future energy manipulation. Why was this the correct sequence of actions? Imagine you have a foreign object stuck in your body. You could start by boosting your immune system, in the hope that it would throw out the foreign object on its own, or you could simply remove the object first and then help the body heal. The solutions from the records are always so simple and elegant. Even after so many years, this never ceases to amaze me.

We performed an energetic cord-cutting ritual, so the energy between Petra and the other woman, which was not of service to either of them, was removed. We did not do this on our own; we asked the masters to do it for Petra. We as people, even if we have the purest intentions, do not know all the details and the soul plans of a human being and thus cannot perform such an operation as successfully as the masters can. It is a bit like a child who has learned where the heart is being allowed to perform open-heart surgery. It won't happen.

Next, the masters told Petra that she needed to strengthen her energy field so no external energies could touch her anymore. The masters led her through a beautiful heart-centered meditation, which showed her how to strengthen her auric field. She was to do this meditation daily until her energy was strong again. The meditation they gave her was specific to her, but if you would like to work on strengthening your own energy field, you can pick any meditation that guides you through focusing on love and expanding the field of your heart. The energy of love is the strongest energy in the universe, and thus the energy of love is the strongest medicine. Last but not least, until Petra was working on strengthening her energy field, she was to create an energetic bubble of protection around herself and her bed at night. This was to help her stay safe while she was working on rebuilding her auric field.

After addressing the biggest issue, the masters moved to addressing Petra's other complaints. They implied that the sleeping problems she had were also due to her entering menopause. Petra confirmed that she had been menopausal for several years (note that we could not see each other; we were on the phone, and I didn't know her age), and this was actually the reason she originally went to the healer for help and advice. The masters explained that a woman does not have to experience unpleasant body reactions when she enters menopause. If her system is in balance, she will not feel any negative consequences in this new phase of life. Just like when winter comes, if we have enough food and heat, we can totally enjoy this new season, in comparison to someone who did not prepare and was left to suffer, hungry and cold. They recommended to Petra to do the following in order to bring back the balance in her body (please note that this advice was specific to her):

- Remove meat and dairy products from her diet. She should eat lots of green vegetables and fruits so that she could increase the alkaline environment in her body.

- Meditate each day. First, spend a week meditating on a regular basis on her third eye chakra by breathing through it (imagining breathing in through the chakra and breathing out through the chakra). This breathing meditation was to balance her energy and her body. After this initial first week, she was to meditate with the rest of the chakras in a similar manner.

- Stop drinking coffee. (Petra claimed that she did not drink lots of coffee. When I pressed her, she said she only drank two to three cups of coffee per day, which was nothing according to her.) The masters explained to her that the coffee causes unnatural body reactions (makes us alert when we are supposed to sleep and rest), which were contraindicative for her. If she wants to enjoy the taste of coffee, she could drink a cup one to two times a week but not daily. They recommended she drink herbal teas instead—green tea in the morning to give her a boost of energy and relaxing tea in the evening.

Note: Please note that the masters give recommendations to everyone individually. Also, please note that a conversation with the records in no way replaces the visit to a certified physician.

Useful Tip: There are many ways to protect oneself energetically, and a bubble of protection is one way to do this. Here is how to do this: imagine a big, glowing balloon around yourself that contains your physical and energetic bodies, even your bed, your bedroom, or your apartment. As we all have free will and are the masters of our reality, the intention that this bubble is there to protect us is enough to keep it in place. Refreshing it from time to time serves to keep it strong and in place. We can infuse it with a specific energy or color that we intuitively feel inspired to do at that moment (e.g., a brilliant blue light). Such energy bubbles we can use not only for protection but also to attract something. We just need to charge them instead with the intention of attracting/keeping something. You can create a bubble and infuse it with beautiful green light for healing or with shimmering pink light for love. The sky is the limit. Let your imagination fly. And last but not least, do it from a place of peace and joy, not from a place of fear and lack. If this is difficult for you to muster, spend some time meditating on love and joy and then create your bubble around you.

※ ※ ※

The Bread Maker

I had a reading once with a lady called Melinda who did not have a specific problem to solve but was simply curious about what the masters would have to tell her. This is a wonderful attitude, because this way we give them the space to tell us what they believe is important for us to know in this moment of our life, and it is often something we did not suspect.

So, we got creative and asked in the Akashic records to be shown a pattern from a past life that influences my client to this present day. The masters showed me the image of bread. I have to admit, I was a bit confused at first. What? Bread? What kind of pattern is this? So, I asked Melinda if she likes eating bread. She said that she does not think she eats too much bread … and she doesn't think much about it. And then she started passionately explaining to me her favorite bread types and from which bakeries in town you can buy them. She has visited them all. She then continued talking about the specifics of making bread, different techniques and ingredients, and the joy it gives her to bake her own bread. I had to laugh. For a person who did not think she had a more special relationship with bread than with other foods, she knew an awful lot about bread. While she was talking, scenes from a past life started unfolding in front of my eyes. The masters showed me that in a past life, Melinda was a baker. They showed me a big, strong, and happy middle-aged man with a huge belly. The baker had his own mill to make flour, and he had turned baking bread into an art. So, OK, obviously the man's passion for bread and baking got transferred into Melinda's life. But was there a problem with that energy? Why were the masters showing us this pattern?

Melinda was gluten intolerant. She loved bread, but she could not eat much of it, and she could eat only special kinds of bread that did not contain wheat. Why was this gluten issue there for Melinda? The masters explained that she needs to learn to have balance in her life; too much of something leads to system overload. Her system was overloaded with wheat from the past life, and this energy was causing her body to reject gluten products in this life. Also, her soul wanted to avoid having her turn her old passion again into a profession; she had other things planned for this life. Melinda was not particularly suffering from her gluten intolerance; it did not bother her much, and she now understood the lessons behind it. The masters invited her to make sure that she kept things in balance throughout her life and did not overdo it on some of the fronts. It is wonderful to have a passion, but it is not worth it if we don't have time to see our family because of it, for example. It is great to have a goal in life but not at the expense of our own health, sleep, and peace.

Useful Tip: I like this particular example because it shows that we don't necessarily need to have experienced a traumatic past life to still feel its influence in our current life. It does not matter if something pleasant or unpleasant happened to us in a past life (or in our more recent current-life past). If we do not let it go and do not learn from it, its energy will continue to be part of our life. This is a topic in many of the spiritual traditions. The Buddhists, for example, talk about nonattachment, and the Christians talk about forgiving and letting go. No matter what our past was, if we continue to carry it on our backs, it will weigh us down. So do not cling to the past and do not wallow in the good old days. Living in the past is not the goal of our existence, and by doing so, we are missing the present.

We need to focus on the current moment and let go of the past if we want to be successful and happy in life.

Similarly, if we worry and think too much about the future, this ultimately gives our subconscious and the universe the signal "I do not believe that I am guided and protected. I am on my own. I need to control things so I can achieve the future I desire." This kind of attitude ultimately means that we do not trust in a loving and caring creator, which makes us feel abandoned, overstressed, and fearful, and this is not a nice place to reside. I know that it can at first be scary to let go of the desire to control every person and event, but it is so worth it. You can make plans, you can have wishes and desires, but then just make sure you are doing the next necessary step to achieve them. And then let go of the thoughts, fears, and hopes for the future. Trust that a trust in the creator and an inspired action are all it takes to live the life of your dreams.

The Village Healer

A gentleman came once to me, Peter, and shared a fascinating story with me. He had a rare health condition. The soft parts of his body—skin, connecting tissue, muscles—were always hurting. He said that he had tried many things, and he currently had the illness under control (he could live normally with the current pain level), but he still felt the pain from time to time. As was to be expected, he wanted to know what the masters and teachers of the Akashic records could tell him about his situation.

A health condition usually is a result of several components that contribute to its manifestation. An event from a past life, an event from the current life, and some unconscious beliefs might be perfect soil for illnesses and other life struggles to flourish. The masters and teachers always show us the root causes of a problem in their descending order of importance—from the most influential one to the least influential one. The masters showed us first a past life of Peter that was linked to his current pains.

In that past life, Peter lived in a medieval village as a woman; the woman was the village healer. Unfortunately, the woman lived in a European village during the Dark Ages, when the religious witch hunts took place. Many souls have suffered from this. I have personally met many healers whose only desire in the past life was to help people, but they were repaid for their kindness by being executed. Such people usually experience physical or psychological issues in their current life; very often they are afraid to express themselves freely, because they fear unconsciously that if they show the world their gifts, something terrible will happen. The woman Peter was in his past life, like many others, was captured by her fellow villagers and sentenced to death by burning at the stake.

The masters depicted a colorful image of the final moments of life of the village healer. She was tied to the stake, the fire was lit, and the flames started dancing and touched and burned first her skin, muscles, and connecting tissues. We have the most pain receptors at our skin; a death by fire is one of the most painful deaths a human being can experience. The shock and the enormous pain were so brutal that the memory of it got transferred from the past life into the current life, manifesting as pain in the exact same places the fire touched first—the skin, muscles, and connecting tissues (the top layer of his body).

Our bodies do have the potential to remain healthy and young for as long as we wish. Most of us, however, do not know what to do in order to remain young and vibrant for a long time, so as time passes, the body starts coming closer to death. The currently normal, natural way for the body to cease its existence is for it to start slowly dying from inside. Our strength decreases, our organs stop working properly, our blood does not run as fast as before. The river of the life force flows slower and slower through us until it can no longer run. Then death occurs. As sad as it might be, this is still a peaceful death. A much more unnatural and painful way for the body to die is when the body dies from the outside (for example, by being burned, shot, or stabbed). In this case, the body and the soul do not have time to prepare for the transition into the next realm, and it can be a very traumatic experience—physically, mentally, and emotionally.

In the records, we find not only the root cause of an issue we have but also the resolution for it. It was time for Peter to heal his old wounds and to be free of the past-life experience. The masters wished for Peter to trigger the healing process during our session. They asked him to take a candle, a thread, and scissors. He was to light the candle (symbolizing the burning stake fires), tie one end of the thread around the candle and the other around his hand (symbolizing the connection between the past and the present lives), and when he was ready for it—to cut the thread connecting the two lives, symbolizing the end of the painful connection between them.

After we finished this ceremony, the masters asked Peter to write down the following points and do them after our session:

- "Perform a ceremony at home." Peter was to take a bowl of water, bless the water with a prayer, and pour the water over himself. The water was the counterpart of the fire, and it had the task of putting the stake fires down.
- "Meditate." For the next few days, Peter was to meditate, imagining pleasantly cold water flowing over his body and through his body, putting down all the fires, calming the tissues, and taking the heat away.
- "Avoid fire Ayurveda foods." For the next several days, Peter was to avoid foods that could feed the fire in him. These are foods that are hot and spicy (a detailed list of the fire Ayurveda foods can be found online or in any Ayurveda book).
- "Forgive." Peter was to do a forgiveness ceremony in which he was to forgive the people from his village for doing what they did, as well as forgiving the world as a whole. It was the world, the era, the times that allowed for such atrocities

to happen. The people themselves were victims of the times they lived in; they simply did not know better. Peter needed to heal his mistrust toward the world and the people in it—healing it with the power of forgiveness.

After completing the discussion on this first issue, we moved to Peter's second issue. He had thyroid problems. The masters answered his question with a question: could he remember when both the thyroid and the body pain issues manifested? They wanted him to make the connection himself and experience an ah-ha moment. Peter remembered that it all happened around his fiftieth birthday, when his focus shifted from his family and career more into his hobbies and calling to be a healer and a spiritual seeker. Indeed, once he decided to go back to the occupation of a healer, the old energies got awoken and bubbled up to the surface to be healed. Similar to the skin pains Peter had, his thyroid issue was connected to this one traumatic past life as the village healer. The masters showed that the woman at the stake wanted to scream from pain, frustration, helplessness, and rage, but unfortunately, she could not complete her cry; it was way too painful. She died before she could complete her scream and swan song. This powerful energy, which needed to go out as the woman's last cry, got stuck in her throat energy center (chakra). Additionally, in Peter's current life, he was supporting this stuck energy by always being the nice guy and not speaking his truth, afraid that he might start a fight. He confirmed that he often swallowed his words in an effort to keep the harmony and peace in a situation. He often kept quiet and to himself. All of these unsaid words and unexpressed feelings were also getting stuck in the throat chakra and multiplying the problem. The thyroid gland resides within the throat chakra. Energy is fluid; it cannot just disappear. If we do not let it flow out, it gets stuck and starts rotting like sewage water, affecting the pipes it is stuck in. Peter had to let that last cry out. He had to express all the unsaid words. The masters asked him to find a time when he was alone at home and then to scream—scream all that out that had accumulated in his throat chakra. Let that last stuck cry out and then promise himself that he would never again swallow his words and keep quiet.

Peter was given a great gift by the masters—the knowledge and understanding of where his problems stemmed from. He was also given the tools to achieve freedom. But his soul still needed to learn its sacred lesson. Peter had to overcome his fear of speaking up. He had to forgive the world and regain his love and trust for people. It was not an easy ask, but it was the way forward for him and for his soul to come into healing.

Useful Tip: Bottling up emotions is never a good idea. We, of course, don't need to express them in a way that might be hurtful to other people, but we need to find a way to let them go. Go in the forest and scream; write a letter and cry your eyes out … and then burn it and let it go; dance like no one is watching; do a forgiveness ceremony; talk to the person who hurt you (or at least to his/her higher self) and clear things out; be authentic and speak your truth. As Buddha says, "Holding on to anger is like grasping a hot coal with the intent of harming another; you are the one who ends up getting burned." It is the same with all other negative emotions; they need to be let go, or they will burn, drown, or choke us … sometimes to death.

A Victim of Religious War

Sandra was a beautiful young woman who came to me one day to ask advice from the Akashic records about an eating disorder she was suffering from. Her entire life, her body had been rejecting the food she was putting in it and making her throw it up. And she loved food! It tasted so good! Unfortunately, the food refused to remain inside Sandra's stomach. There were only a few things that she could swallow and keep in her stomach—tomatoes and cheese. It was not a psychological condition she had, according to her doctors, but rather a strange physical one, which so far remained undiagnosed and unresolved. Sandra had been surviving on the few nutrients her body could extract before it rejected the food. She could digest and process fully very few products and lots and lots of vitamins and supplements. After trying everything she could think of and visiting an endless string of doctors, she was almost ready to give up. I opened the records and asked what the cause of Sandra's condition was.

Immediately, a vivid scene unfolded in front of my eyes. I was shown a woman lying on a dirty street, starving to death. There was chaos around her, howling people, swirling seas of flies, and many other dead bodies. It was a gruesome scene, and it seemed it was Sandra's past life. In this past life, Sandra lived as a woman, and this woman died of hunger. To explain better the connection between the past life and Sandra's current condition, the masters gave us the example of a person who did not have food for a long time, and his bodily functions were already starting to shut off. If such a person is fed an abundance of food, the body will reject it, even though it desperately needs it; a special procedure is needed to gently reintroduce food to the body so it will not get overwhelmed by the food intake. Sandra's current body was in a similar situation. The energy imprint of a starving body got carried over from her past life to her present one. Her body was in a locked state of impending death by starvation.

It is not as important how we die as it is in what state we die. Our thoughts, feelings, emotions, and promises at the moment of our death, if too strong for the spirit to let go of, get stuck and transferred to our next lifetimes. If we die in peace and are able to forgive, we will have less karmic energy to work through in our next reincarnation. However, if we die in pain, full of disappointment, hatred, resentment, and bitterness, these feelings can remain imprinted onto us, pulling us into a next reincarnation, where we will have time to deal with them. Therefore, religions speak of forgiveness and have special rituals for freeing the spirit before and after the moment of death.

Once Sandra managed to digest (pun intended) the initial message from the masters, they showed us why Sandra's death was so emotional for her and why her spirit was not able to forgive and let go of the circumstances. The city in which the starving woman lived was one of the old Muslim cities in Asia (Sandra was a Muslim in her current life too). A few weeks before her death, the city got surrounded by Christian crusaders who demanded the population convert to Christianity. In truth, it seemed that this was rather an excuse the crusaders used to simply ravage through the cities in the area. People were scared and refusing to leave the city gates. At first, the crusaders attacked the city with fire, but the city walls were thick and unbreakable. This enraged the soldiers, and they set the city under long-lasting occupation; no provisions were to enter or leave the city gates. The people started to starve, and death slowly crept into the city. First the kids and the weak and sick people started to die, and then the stronger adults followed. The city was dying a slow, painful, and emotional death. People were praying on the streets to their God, but their prayers remained unanswered. The occupation continued. The hunger drove some people mad. Brother was stealing food from brother. A sister was killing a sister to get her hands on some food. Some people even started attacking fellow citizens in order to kill and eat them. It was a nightmare hard to imagine. The woman Sandra used to be in that past life was also attacked by her family. They stole her food and chased her away. Scared, hungry, crying, alone, betrayed, and disappointed in everyone and everything, the woman died on the streets, cursing her fate, her God, and her loved ones.

Sandra was in tears. We both could feel the pain of the dead woman, her disappointment and her rage. Dying a death infused with such intense emotions was bound to have its consequences. We understood why her body was still suffering the symptoms of a starving body. What was even more interesting was what Sandra shared with me at this point of our conversation. She told me that she was quite annoyed by her current mother and brother. According to her, they were jealous of her and her financial success, and whenever they came to her place, they stole food from her fridge, despite them being quite well financially themselves. The masters confirmed that some of her current family was her family in her past life too. Sandra needed to resolve not only the trauma of her body but also the karma created between her and her loved ones if she wanted to have a lighter, happier, better life.

The biggest reason for Sandra's current suffering, however, was the chasm that was created between her and the divine. The woman who died believing God abandoned her, cursing him and denoting him, was now in great pain. There is no bigger wound than our separation from God and our (faulty) belief that he has abandoned us, that he doesn't even exist, or even worse—that he has actually never really loved us or cared about us.

The masters ensured Sandra that what she was experiencing was not God's wrath. We might think that God abandons us or gets angry at us, but this could not be further from the truth. God has only unconditional love for us and being loved unconditionally means we will be loved regardless of what we do, think, or say. If nothing else, I hope this book teaches you at least this.

One question people often ask is, "How can a loving God let me suffer like this?" This is a fair question, but it is also a question that demonstrates the lack of understanding of how the universe works. God is not letting us suffer; God is letting us experience life. Taking one's own life is in many religions depicted as a bigger crime than murder. Why? Because committing suicide is rejecting the sacred gift of life, destroying the precious gem that has been entrusted to you to care for. So, do you get punished if you take your own life? No, you do not, but your soul might decide to get reborn in a situation where it will learn the value of life, and this might be a painful lesson for a human being to go through. God only wishes for us to be whole, to feel loved, and to be happy—and this can only fully happen when we finally remerge with God again. And it is our choice how and when we will achieve this.

People say, "OK, why am I choosing this? I do not want to suffer. I choose to end all this nonsense and return straight to God!" In this case, I often give as an example a trip to an exotic, interesting, and exciting but underdeveloped country. Many people chose to travel to such a country, even though it is possible they will get mugged, infected by some disease, even raped or murdered. Others choose to delve into extreme sports that could also quite bring the end of their life. Yes, such endeavors could be quite dangerous, but we choose to do them anyway. Why? Because we like adventures, because we want to challenge ourselves, because we want to experience something new and expand our knowledge and understanding of the world. It is the same with our souls. A soul knows the risks it takes when taking upon a particular life here on earth, but it does it despite all the risks, because all the benefits outweigh all the negatives. Actually, for a soul to reincarnate on earth is a rather easy, no-brainier decision compared to a human being going to a dangerous country. The soul can never die; it knows that at the end of the day, nothing bad can happen to it, because it is eternal, immortal. It is a piece of God.

Sandra was ready to let go of the past. Her current suffering was so unbearable that the pain was a strong enough convincer for her to do whatever it took to free herself from it—even forgive what some might think unforgivable. She had much forgiveness work to do if she wanted to resolve her current issues with her family and around food. My client needed to forgive the Christian crusaders who attacked her city; she needed to forgive the people who were her family back then and also now; she needed to forgive and make peace with God.

What followed surprised me but also brought deep healing in my own heart. The energy of the Akashic records flows through the channeler during a session, so I am bound to be part of the healing process of my clients—a healing that affects us both. A forgiveness needed to be asked for and given for the pain inflicted by the Christian soldiers. As I am born Christian, the masters decided to use me and Sandra to bring peace between these two religions. It was a quite emotional moment for us both when the masters told me that I should ask forgiveness from Sandra in the name of the Christians for all the pain they had caused the Muslims. We both burst into tears when we heard the master's request. There is so much accumulated pain in our societies from all the centuries-long, senseless quarrels between the two religions. An eye for an eye … leaves the world blind. We felt this pain and were ready to let it go. I offered Sandra my apology as a Christian, and she gracefully received it as a Muslim; then she asked for forgiveness of me for the pain Muslims have inflicted on Christians. The cycle was complete for us. Sandra felt lighter.

The first step toward Sandra's healing was done. Then the masters proceeded to the rest of Sandra's homework. They asked her to do the following:

- Focus on a strictly vegan diet for a given period of time—no meat, fish, eggs, milk, or cheese. Her body needed alive food and many good nutrients.
- Eat each bite slowly, with extreme joy and gratitude for the abundance that was on her table now.
- Every time she was to eat something, Sandra was to ask her body if it wanted to receive it. Sandra could use her body as a pendulum and let it tilt toward the food if it was a yes and away from the food if it was a no. The masters told her to take this answer on a case-by-case basis, as it was very much possible that her body needed a particular food at one time and not at another.
- Make a list of the resources she had (money, clothes, time, etc.) and decide what her needs were for living a comfortable

and abundant life. She was allowed to give to others only after she had an overflow of her own resources.

- Every morning, she was to offer her gratitude to God for being alive.

The last advice the masters gave Sandra was the most important one. She needed to forgive God. The masters asked her to write a letter that she did not need to show or send to anyone but could burn when she was ready for it. In this letter, she was to pour out all her emotions and pain, feeling free to curse whoever and whatever she wanted, but to then finish the letter with forgiveness for her loved ones and for God. Sandra did not need to immediately start writing this letter or to even finish writing it in one sitting. But she needed to do it for the poison to leave her system and be released by the fire. Fire attacked her city in the past, and fire was to purify her heart now.

Useful Tip: The masters very often give the advice to people to use their bodies as a pendulum when deciding if they should eat a certain food or not, as well as if they should continue eating or not. This advice can be used by people who want to lose weight, people who have mysterious food-related conditions, or simply if you want to make sure you keep your body healthy. We try to solve our problems by attacking them from outside, with logic and force, while often the solution is inside—using our intuition and turning toward our own body for the answer.

Put the food in front of your solar plexus and quiet your body and mind. Ask your body if you should eat this food now or not. Wait for the answer—your body will sway either forward or backward. Allow for it to happen; don't control it. If your body moves toward the food—eat it, if it moves away from it—leave it to the side for now and feed your body something else. Be respectful of the needs of your body and honor its wisdom.

※ ※ ※

There Is a Ghost in My Apartment

I do not know anyone who does not believe in ghosts at least a little bit. And usually the people who refuse to talk about ghosts are most afraid of them. Since I started working with the Akashic records, I know for sure that there are many spirits and energies around us. Some are there to love and support us, while others are there because they need something and hope to get it through us. It is always our decision if we will allow a presence to remain around us or not (we need to be aware of our power and sovereignty). We have been granted the gift of free will, and as such, we are the masters of our life and our reality. Nothing and no one has the right or the power to overrule our decision, especially when we explicitly state our intention.

One of the first cases I got when I started giving Akashic records readings was with Eveline. She came to me quite scared and said that she was afraid to live in her apartment and was wondering if there was a ghost living there. She explained that she heard weird noises, things fell on the floor without an apparent reason, and (the freakiest of all) she woke up often at night, completely stiff and unable to move, with the strong feeling that something was trying to enter her body. Eveline had taken a long time to find her current apartment. It was the perfect location, price, and size for her, and that was why, before taking the final step of moving out because of the ghost, she came to me, in the hope she could keep on living in her dream home.

I opened Eveline's Akashic records and asked the masters and teachers if there was indeed a ghost in Eveline's apartment or if her experiences were based on something else. Yes, they said, there was indeed a ghost there. But Eveline did not need to be afraid of the being. The masters explained that before Eveline moved into the flat, there was an old lady who lived there for more than thirty years. The lady died, but her ghost was still very much attached to the apartment. Eveline confirmed that it was the mother of her landlord who lived in the apartment before her and who actually died in there; that was also one of the reasons why the apartment was being rented for such a low price. Before telling Eveline how she could get rid of the ghost, the masters wanted to awaken compassion and understanding in her for the deceased old lady. They told her that the mother of her landlord did not understand that she had died; she believed that she was still alive and was furious that Eveline had invaded her space! Imagine how you would react if somehow a stranger started living in your home! The poor lady was trying to communicate and yell (strange noises), throw things around (things falling down), and push the intruder out of the house (Eveline feeling that someone was trying to enter her body).

These explanations relaxed my client a bit. It seemed that she was not going crazy, and there was indeed a ghost in her apartment, which was not some evil spirit but a scared and confused (and a bit angry) old lady. Eveline had been given the chance to assist a spirit to let go of its earthly life and to continue on its path into the light, beyond the plane of the living. If anything, this interaction between the two women was a blessing for them both; one was to get help on her spirit journey, and the other had the chance to expand her knowledge, love, and compassion. Here is what the masters asked Eveline to do:

- Go home and talk to the old lady. Explain to her that she was unfortunately already dead, that Eveline had rented the apartment from her son and was living legally there. Also, Eveline was to promise the old lady that she would take a good care of her apartment and her furniture.
- The masters explained to Eveline what is usually there for the spirit to see after the body dies—a light, an opening above (like an opened door, from which streams soft, comforting, loving light), where many beautiful beings wait to welcome the deceased—angels, guides, and many deceased loved ones. It was a beautiful picture, a map, that Eveline was to explain to the old lady, then ask her to look for this light and

go there whenever she felt ready for it. Many spirits seem to be so focused on the earthly events that they do not think about looking up and thus remain unaware of their next step—the light to the next dimension waiting for them.

- Leave biscuits on a nice plate on the balcony. The masters told Eveline that the cookies were to serve as a symbol for peace offering. It was also similar to the ritual where relatives give out food as part of the funeral procedures when a person dies. When a person dies, food needs to be part of the sending-off rituals. It is related to our link to the material and earthly plane. The masters told Eveline to imagine it like the final meal of the deceased before the spirit leaves this material plane for good—one last enjoyment of the earthly pleasures.

Eveline was very excited to go home and perform the rituals. The masters told Eveline that this should take care of the ghost but that she was actually somebody who was sensitive to the finer energies and to the energies of deceased spirits. Somebody else would have remained blind and deaf to the actions of the old lady's ghost. They reminded Evelin that she was the one still living on the material plane, and she was the master of her body and her life. Her free will could not be broken by anybody else in the universe. They advised her that if at some point a spirit tried to contact her again and tried to enter her body, she did not need to be afraid but simply state that this was her body and her space, and the being was to leave immediately.

A few weeks later, I got a call from Eveline. She was more than happy and quite excited. She said she did everything that the masters advised her to do, and since then, she had not had any more troubles with the spirit of the old lady. What surprised her even more was that shortly after her talk with the lady ghost, a wooden cabinet cover came off by itself, and she found their old family photos. Eveline collected and packed the photos gently and sent them to her landlord—the son of the deceased lady. It seemed that the ghost understood that Evelin was the new good-hearted tenant of the flat and asked her for a favor. But what made Eveline call me was a conversation she had with a neighbor that day. The neighbor told her that the old lady loved having her afternoon coffee on the balcony … with biscuits. I felt goose bumps; the masters always manage to leave me speechless. They knew that the lady loved to eat biscuits on her balcony and that would have been the perfect peace offering. My heart melts and a smile comes to my face every time I think about this story … and when I enjoy my own afternoon tea biscuits.

Useful Tip: If you are having issues with a friendly or not so friendly spirit, do not despair. There are many approaches to send a foreign energy away. The most effective way is to do it with love, wishing the best to this person or being. It is essential to understand that a person (dead or alive) goes for hurting others only when they have been hurt themselves. That is why the most efficient way to free yourself of a foreign, unwanted presence is not to forcefully push it out of your space but to lovingly facilitate the healing for both of you. In this way, the resolution will be much more permanent, and it will be done in the name of the highest good of all.

There are several reasons why a foreign energy can be felt by you: it is directly related to you and wants to communicate something to you; it is in no way family related to you, but it feels that you can help it; it found a weakness of yours and is trying through you to fill a gap in itself. Regardless the reason, this energy is actually looking for love and healing. And there is no more perfect team to guide and assist in this than the loving and powerful masters of the Akashic records.

The Boy Who Was Afraid of Blood

A young man, Jorge, came to me one day. He was in his twenties and said that he had a problem he would like to tackle. He was afraid of blood. But he was not always afraid of blood. His fear kicked in only when he thought the blood was spilled for a sad reason (e.g., someone got hurt). He said if he knew that something was being done for the good of the bleeding person, he was fine with seeing the blood. When he donated blood once, he had no problem seeing it. But when he saw his own blood when he got a paper cut, or when he saw blood in a thriller movie, he was almost hysterical.

I entered his Akashic records and asked the masters what they could tell us about his troubles. Immediately a scene from a past life emerged—a man lying on the ground, bleeding out to death, surrounded by the bloody, still warm corpses of his dead and dying fellow villagers. The man had died in a bloodbath. The scene was from the Middle Ages in Europe. These kinds of events were not unusual for those times. There were many bandits and fights for power between the settlements and the small and big kingdoms. The masters explained to us, however, that Jorge, in his past reincarnation, was the village healer and as such was responsible for predicting future events and taking care of his village. He obviously had failed miserably in his task. He did not predict the attack on the village. He was not able to save his people. He died surrounded by the blood and distorted bodies of his fellow villagers with a burning guilt, bitterness, and doubt in his own abilities in his heart. His current fear of blood was a reflection of the deep emotional trauma he experienced at the moment of his past-life death.

Until this moment, Jorge had usually seen blood flowing out of a body as something bad (referencing the scene of his past life—blood flowing out the bodies of the dying people around him). The masters challenged him to look at blood and the human body as highly intelligent. In some cases, when there was danger for the internal organs, the blood could rush toward them. In such a moment, even if you cut yourself, very little blood would bleed out of the wound. So the blood can move toward the places where it is needed, making the blood a hero and not a villain to be feared. Blood flowing out of a wound is something good that happens. If a person cuts himself, the blood rushes toward the wound because it wants to nurture the cells of the cut. It wants to disinfect and heal and close the wound. The act of bleeding is actually a beautifully designed mechanism of the body to self-heal and take care of itself. So, in effect, seeing blood appear could just as well be celebrated and revered, because the body is doing its job perfectly. The flowing blood is not the reason for the person's suffering; the blood is helping to ease it. The masters urged Jorge next time he gets a paper cut to talk to the blood and thank it for its wonderful service, and when he was ready, to also look at it and thank it face-to-face.

But the fear of blood was not the most crucial problem Jorge had. The masters used this topic and opportunity as a trampoline to speak to him about something that was crippling him much more than the fear of blood was. What they were referring to was his fear of stepping into his own power. Disappointed at his own "incompetency" in the past life, Jorge subconsciously did not trust his skills in the current life. He admitted that he was indeed quite a shy person who was reluctant to push forward in life. This was of course no surprise, knowing the history of his soul. In that past life, his abilities were not enough to warn and protect his fellow villagers. People died because he was "incapable," so now Jorge was afraid to even try.

Hearing these explanations helped my client relax. He got validation that there was a good reason for his fears. It was not a reason from this life, but it still was a very valid reason. Now he was ready to hear the masters' suggestions about how to release the trauma from the past.

The masters encouraged him to do a few small initial steps and to try to put himself out there. There was no other way out of his inner hell than straight through the fires. He needed to stop being afraid of the fear. They promised him that they would be with him every step of the way and that they knew he was a very capable and good-hearted young man. In addition to encouraging him, they proposed to him a meridian-tapping energy healing technique (also known as EFT). Our emotions can get stuck in our energy system, and no matter how vigorously we try to convince ourselves to act a certain way, our unconscious patterns make us act a different way.

The masters pointed out to Jorge what unconscious patterns he had—the fear that he was incapable—explained to him where this pattern had come from (the past life), and gave him a technique for how to release it (meridian tapping). It is important to know that the way our soul and our subconscious work is not flawed. It was no mistake that the energy from the past life got transferred as a trauma and an unconscious belief in his current life. Jorge's soul needed to prove to itself that what happened was not his fault; he needed to forgive himself and to heal the anger in himself toward people who hurt others. This was a task his soul consciously picked for his currenly life and now he had the chance to resolve it.

Useful Tip: It happens often that we have one problem and look for help with it, but the masters, in their unconditional love for us, direct us toward an even deeper problem we have. In the case of Jorge, we did address his issue with seeing blood, but we actually delved deeper into the topic of him not thinking he is good enough, which was preventing him to succeed in life. The inability to believe in himself was transferred from his past life, but it was also reinforced in his childhood (being mobbed and ridiculed at high school, being rather a loner). It often happens this way. A karmic experience gets reawaken in childhood, as to initiate the turning of the wheels in this lifetime. In that sense, it would be possible to address the issue working only with the childhood negative experiences Jorge had and so build up his confidence, but in our case, we addressed it via going back to its actual root cause—the events in his past life. If you think you need help, do look for it. The universe is a loving place, and there are many methods, wonderful people, and therapists out there who are ready to help you. You do not need to look for the perfect tool or person. You do not need to wait for the perfect moment. You just need to make the first (or the next) step, and step by step, you will reach your end goal and be healed and free. It is not always an easy and pleasant journey, but it is a journey very much worth taking.

※ ※ ※

Chopping an Arm Off

A friend of mine, Elizabeth, came to me once with the complaint of pain in her right arm. The pain was not very strong, but it was always there and was uncomfortable. The physicians Elizabeth visited told her that there was nothing wrong with her arm and the pain might be psychologically based. Born and raised in a good and loving family, never having her heart broken, never having been physically attacked, never having experienced a big trauma, and living a happy and balanced life, Elizabeth was at a loss as to what the psychological reason could be. We decided to ask in the Akashic records and see if there was some information that could help her.

The masters showed me an image of one of Elizabeth's past lives. In this past life, she was a strong young man—the most influential and revered man in the village, almost a giant. In the same village lived a woman of untold beauty, and the young man saw it fit that she was to belong to him. His ego told him that the strongest man should have the most beautiful woman. The village beauty, however, was in love with another man. When our hero found out about it, he was enraged. His ego got deeply wounded, and he decided to do what every self-respecting man of that era would do—to attack and kill his rival and take the woman for himself. It was an uneven battle, and the young man beat the other one so severely that he almost killed him. When the time of the final blow came, he did not find it in himself to kill his fellow villager. "Here is your wedding gift," he said and snapped the right arm of his rival. "May every time you embrace her, you remember me and fear fill up your heart." The two lovers married, and the strong young man grew old and bitter; everyone feared him, and no woman dared to love him. He died having his fair share of power and the respect of his fellows but without the chance to love and be loved. He was cursing his fate, the beautiful woman, and her chosen one. The arm of the one man had long healed, but the heart and the hurt ego of the other one never did. The arm that hurt Elizabeth was the same arm the young man cut of his fellow villager.

After depicting this grim story, the masters proceeded to explain to Elizabeth that the pain she was currently suffering from was in no way a form of punishment for what she had done in her past life as the powerful and bitter man. For they said that her soul had learned the lesson of the past life and was free of grudges and unresolved emotions. It chose, however, to keep the pain in the arm as a reminder for Elizabeth to continue working on her temper and her ego.

Overcoming our ego is a task each one of us has. It is not a complicated task, but it definitely is not an easy one. In order to live free of ego and pride, instead of focusing on what others have and what they might think of us, we need to turn our focus inward instead. Comparing ourselves to others brings us nothing good. We keep on fighting in the outside world to get that which we desire, but the real battle is within. Competing with others feeds our ego and brings us only sorrow; competing with ourselves in our effort to reach God brings us humility and freedom.

Of course, the masters never leave you hanging there with information without offering you advice on how to resolve the issue. And as the masters are, they offered Elizabeth a very gentle and effective solution to let go of the pain in her arm: a ceremony of flowers and water.

For the ceremony, Elizabeth was invited to take a big bowl of water and many flowers. She was to put a flower in the bowl for every big or small hurt she had received or inflicted in this lifetime. "Why water and why flowers?" Elizabeth asked. Because the water has the power to cleanse and neutralize the energies, explained the masters, and to bring everything back to balance. And the flowers? Because each one of us is a beautiful flower in the garden of God, and we make the world a more wonderful place through our existence. A flower represented a piece of a human soul that felt hurt.

After putting all the flowers in the bowl, Elizabeth was asked to speak to the flowers and ask them for forgiveness. For every pain she inflicted, she was to ask forgiveness of this person during the ceremony. And for every pain that was inflicted on her, she was to ask forgiveness of herself, because she left herself open to be hurt. Elizabeth had to also ask forgiveness from the soul of that man she fought in her past life, and she was also to give herself forgiveness for what she had done. By hurting another being, she had actually hurt herself. She brought upon herself a past life filled with bitterness and sorrow and a pain that got transferred into her current life as a reminder to not repeat the same mistake. Elizabeth was to speak to the flowers for as long as she needed, asking for and giving forgiveness, allowing all the hurts to flow out of her and into the bowl of water. And when all words were said and all tears were spilled, she was to take that bowl of water and flowers and pour its contents in her garden. At a funeral, you let go of the past, because the past is no more, and you bury the remains of the person in the earth so their energy can get purified and transformed. At a funeral, you also bring flowers. By ending the ceremony that way, Elizabeth showed the universe that she was ready to bury and let go of all of her old wounds, putting flowers on their graves. Are the lords of the Akashic records not poets and masters of energy work? I think they are. And so was Elizabeth. Soon after, the pain in her arm disappeared.

Useful Tip: Dissolving karma is easily done by letting go, giving and receiving forgiveness, and embracing the situation with love. To give and receive forgiveness, you do not need the other person to be present. Your own emotions create your life, karma, and experiences. When you are ready to forgive and when you are ready to be forgiven, this is all the universe needs to return the energies around you back to balance. There are many ways to forgive: you can write a letter, pouring your emotions into it (and later burn it, or bury it, or send it off on a river); you can perform a ceremony of forgiveness, like the one Elizabeth did; you can make a list of all the people you feel you have forgiveness work to do with and use Ho'oponopono with each one of them; you can pray and let God do the rest. Regardless of what approach you choose, forgiveness is a powerful tool to resolve one of the biggest issues you might have in life.

A Complex Life Story Turns Simple

The last story I would like to tell you is of a reading that touched many different topics in the client's life, which turned out to be all linked to the same root cause—Joe's feeling of worthlessness and lack of self-love and self-respect.

It happens often that we have multiple seemingly unrelated problems that all stem from the same energy and behavior pattern. Your character determines how you interact with the world, and how you interact with the world determines how your relationships, career, and all other areas of life will look. It is usually the case that at a particular moment of our lifetime, we struggle with a specific lesson, and this lesson is the silver lining between all our current issues. We can imagine it like a math skill. Until a student learns addition and subtraction, she will fail any tasks in geometry, trigonometry, fractals, and so on. The solution of any future math problem depends on the mastery of the previous skills. It is not a punishment that we cannot progress in life until we learn a particular life lesson; it is just how life works. Even if you were allowed to pass to the next level, despite not learning the lessons from the previous one, your life would not become easier but harder! If we allow third graders into the university lecture halls, the poor children will have enormous stress and will very quickly give up. So, it is for our own good that until we learn a particular skill, we will not be able to progress further in life.

Joe came to me one day with a bag full of complaints. To be honest, I was at a loss when he started enumerating his issues. For the past several months, Joe was having speech, memory, and balance difficulties. He was suffering from panic attacks and intense fear of death. He was bursting into sudden episodes of rage; his palms were sweating; he was feeling pressure in his chest; and he had occasional cramps all over his body. And he desperately wanted to get rid of it all. I waited patiently for Joe to finish listing his troubles. I knew that even if this list did sound quite overwhelming to me, the masters would know what to do with it. I opened Joe's records, and we asked what the cause of his symptoms was.

The answer that came from the masters surprised me. It was a poltergeist, they said, whose presence was triggering all these sensations for Joe. Joe was a bit at a loss with this answer. He said that no relative or friend of his had recently passed away. The masters insisted that this was the reason for his symptoms. The ghost was not related to Joe but was rather attached to the property where Joe was living. This lit a bulb for Joe. He confirmed that several months ago, he indeed moved to a new flat; he never made the connection before between his new flat and the appearance of his problems, but now he could see that his symptoms all started shortly after he moved in.

I always giggle internally when something like this happens. We as humans are usually so immersed in our lives that we lose sight of the big picture and miss obvious cause-effect connections. The masters see everything from a totally different perspective and are happy to point us in the right direction. Actually, "absurd" answers like "The cause for your difficulty with balance is an angry ghost who is pushing you around" are a clear sign for any new practitioner working with the records that the channeled information is authentic. Our logical brains would never come up with such far-fetched, "crazy" answer, and our fragile ego would never allow us to say something so "laughable."

The masters continued their explanation. Joe's ghost friend was an old man who used to live in the house but had died some one hundred years ago. What was so special about this ghost? He was very bitter and angry. You might wonder if this ghost had been there for more than one hundred years, why did no one else do anything to calm him down? Many would actually rather run away than deal with it, but most simply do not feel anything. The spirit energy is very fine, and unless we are sensitive to it, we will not notice it. This very year, Joe had purposefully started to sharpen his senses because he wanted to grow spiritually and wanted to learn to work with fine energies. But the things he felt shortly after starting his new hobby were quite intense, and this scared him, so Joe decided to stop honing these new skills. The path of spirit, however, is the path where our soul wants to lead us, and once we step on it, we cannot unlearn it. Joe put himself unknowingly in an unideal situation. He did not have a teacher to ask for advice about working with energy, and he did not continue his studies to look for a proper way to deal with his newly opened energy channels. The masters explained this to Joe with the following example: A blind man is holding the tail of an elephant for many years and following the elephant around. One day, after trying very hard for a very long time, he finally manages to cure his eyes and open this new sense—sight. When the blind man opened his eyes, he saw the huge elephant and freaked out! He had never before seen an elephant! He tried to close his eyes again, but he could not unsee the elephant, and he could not return to blindness. Also, there was no other person around to explain to the newly healed man that this elephant is no monster from hell but simply a normal animal. So, Joe had seen the elephant and was holding his eyes shut now in the hope that it would all go back to normal again. But just as sight is an amazing sense to have, so is the sense of intuition and feeling energy. It is a gift, not a curse. We just need to learn a few things about how to navigate it.

So, Joe's new sensitivity to energy was the reason he felt the presence of the ghost. And his unwillingness to continue walking the spiritual path he had stepped on had prevented him from finding a solution sooner. Joe's body was unable to deal with the presence of the unfriendly ghost, resulting in the myriad of unpleasant symptoms. There were two possible things Joe could do to resolve his issue with his not so friendly poltergeist. He could move to a different house, or he could face his fears and help himself and the ghost find peace. The masters did not push Joe toward a particular decision. It was his life and his free will how to live it. But the wiser decision was to stay and deal with the situation. This is what Joe went for. The masters gave him the following steps to follow, in order, to deal with the ghost energy:

1. Create an energetic protection around himself so the ghost does not bother him anymore. This energetic protection, interestingly, had to be a necklace with a cross, or an icon next to Joe's bed, or some other religious object, which had to be blessed by a priest in a church.

2. Write a letter to this ghost (speaking directly to the ghost would have been too scary for Joe). In this letter, Joe was to explain to the ghost that he was dead, Joe was alive, this was Joe's house now, and it was time for the ghost to look up and move into the light.

3. Make a donation or another act of service to the church (any particular church or the church as an organization).

4. Light a candle in the window, as light illuminates the path of the soul.

5. Go to a graveyard (any graveyard, as Joe did not know where the old man was buried) and leave flowers there, thus showing respect, love, and compassion for the deceased man.

These steps sounded quite strange and uncomfortable for Joe. He was not a religious person and even had a slight aversion toward the church institution. The masters explained to him why the steps were as they were. These acts were not to heal Joe but to help the ghost heal. The deceased man was a highly religious man when he was alive, and religious symbols and rituals had a very deep meaning for him. The man had died however in a quarrel with the church. He died bitter and angry and could not forgive himself. Here came step three from above—do an act of service for the church. Joe was to do this act in the name of the dead man—a final act of love and service toward his beloved church and religion, an act of apology and making peace. God does not judge us, but we do judge ourselves, and if we believe we transgressed, we try to fix it. The ghost could see the light that was waiting for him, but he did not believe he was worthy to go into the light. He thought that he had committed a grave sin and was afraid to face God and the afterlife, so he remained on earth, angry, sad, scared, and hateful. The masters have unconditional love for each one of us. The information and the solutions we receive from them are always for the highest good of us all. They wanted to help both Joe and the soul of the dead man.

Some weeks later, I got an email from Joe. He did follow the steps the masters gave him, and he could no longer feel the presence of the ghost. His symptoms had disappeared with time, and he was feeling happy and content in his new apartment. Not only that, Joe managed to find some peace and come to terms with the church institution.

This was a very rich reading. Joe was full of questions, and the masters were full of answers for him. When we completed this first question of Joe's, he had another one. His eyesight had been getting noticeably worse in the past couple of months. The masters and teachers in the records told him that it was not related to his ghost friend this time, but it was related to his mother and her unhappiness with how Joe was living his life. Joe was again not having good energy boundaries (like in the case of the ghost) and was allowing another person's energy to penetrate his space and influence him physically and emotionally.

One interesting thing about the work with the masters and teachers in the records is that they are amazingly efficient. They have in mind your soul evolution and see no point in you wasting one lifetime after another in order to learn one lesson when a fast and direct path exists for you to learn this same lesson here and now—if you are willing to do the necessary work. By now, you might have started noticing that on the outside, Joe's issues were very different, and the underlying root causes were different, but what the masters told Joe as a conclusion of the session was that he needed to work on his boundaries, his self-esteem, and his self-respect. He had close to zero self-respect and was allowing everybody in his life to walk all over him. This is a very unhealthy way to be and was opening many channels for foreign energies to enter Joe's space and influence him. The masters told Joe to do some mirror work. Every day, a few times a day, for a few months he was to look into his eyes in a mirror and tell himself how amazing, wonderful, awesome, and strong he is. Joe had to believe in his own strength. Then no foreign energy could penetrate his field. The masters basically taught him how to build his energy immune system, which had the task of rejecting any approaching foreign energy.

Joe had one last question. He had epilepsy since he was a child. He had a surgery, and things had been going quite well after it (a big shout-out to the amazing doctors and nurses!), but he was still having a few seizures from time to time. The masters and teachers told him that this was coming from a past life Joe had. In this past life, he killed a man by hitting him on the head, and this energy got so strongly imprinted into the ether that Joe was feeling the aftereffects of it in his current lifetime. The masters recommended Joe do forgiveness work—ask the soul of the man he killed for forgiveness, give forgiveness himself to anyone who might have hurt him, and also forgive himself. You can imagine that Joe, who on some subconscious level was considering himself a killer and brought with him the painful memory of the murder in the form of brain epilepsy, did not have a very high opinion of himself and a very high self-esteem. Going back to the mirror work, self-love, and acceptance, the universe does not judge us; we are our only judges.

The masters showed Joe how loved he actually is and encouraged him to find his lost value. And after all, who are we to consider ourselves unworthy when we are a piece of God? Are we calling God unworthy? A bit arrogant of us, don't you think?

Useful Tip: The masters often recommend to people to work with a mirror in order to build their self-love and self-esteem. What does it mean to work with a mirror? Look into a mirror. It can be big or small. You can see just your face or your entire body. You can stand in front of it naked or fully clothed. Try out different things. However, the one thing that remains constant in this exercise are the words you tell yourself, and these are words of deep love and appreciation: "I love you so much. You are so amazing. I am always here for you. You did so well in that meeting yesterday. Oh my, I love those hips. What beautiful, deep eyes you have. I love myself. I am amazing." The world is your oyster. Use your imagination for how to love yourself and see your self-love and self-respect skyrocket.

How do you know if this exercise is for you? If you think it's stupid, it's for you. If you feel uncomfortable even reading about it, it's for you. If you get excited by the idea, it's for you. It is an exercise that can benefit each one of us. We are like the flowers in a garden; we always need another dose of water and sunlight—a.k.a. love and appreciation. For as long as we live, we will need it, so we might as well just give it to ourselves in abundant dosages. We are children of the love and light. We can never get too much of it, and too little of it can make us think life is not worth living.

You might think that doing this is too egoistic or too narcissistic. Well … it is not. The masters very often show my clients the following image: hungry people walking the world, trying to get some nourishment from others, versus satisfied people walking the world, feeling inspired to give to others. We all have needs—the need to eat food and drink water but also the need to love and feel loved. If we do not get our needs met, we feel undernourished, and we do everything possible to find that which we need. However, we are often taught that it is egoistic to first think about ourselves, so we don't, and thus we turn our focus outwardly and as a consequence start to expect others to nourish us. But nobody knows our needs and desires as well as we do, and nobody can meet them as well as we ourselves can. This leads to a world of undernourished and cranky people who are angry with their family and friends, feel unsatisfied with life, and go around like unconscious vampires, looking for their next fix.

On the other hand, imagine a world where each one of us is wise and responsible enough to first nurture our needs and then go out into the world. This will lead to a world of happy, satisfied people who do not hold the others responsible for their own happiness but who genuinely like to connect with other people—not because they need something but because they enjoy it and have surplus to offer.

So, you see, we've got it all wrong. Taking care of our needs for love, attention, and appreciation is anything but egoistic; it is the most altruistic thing we can do for the world, because then we will face each one with a smile on our face and not with a hidden agenda.

Go get a mirror now and spend some time with the most important person in your life—you.

The masters make only one exception to this rule—the case where you have little children. Then you are allowed to put their needs before yours, but still not always and definitely not for long, uninterrupted periods. No one likes a cranky mom who shouts at her kids because she's exhausted and hungry. So, if you have kids, do take care of them, but also make sure you pay attention to yourself and are the best version you could be—for their and your own sake.

CHAPTER 4

Conversations with God and the Masters

With man this is impossible, but with God all things are possible.
—Matthew 19:26

In the Akashic records, you can ask to speak directly with each one of the masters and teachers. If it will serve your highest purpose, they will appear and interact with you. You can speak directly with archangel Michael, archangel Gabriel, Jesus Christ, Buddha, Mother Mary, and any other being of light you can think of. No matter who you call, the main message and answer to your questions will be the same, but depending on which being you speak with, you will feel the energy of his/her personality, and the message will be infused with his/her specific vibration. It is a beautiful feeling—just like speaking with different people on earth. Each one of them has their personal qualities and specific character. I love conversing with the masters; it is such a blessing to be able to consciously be in the company of these light beings. And this is possible for you, too, if you so wish. The keys to the Akashic records have been handed to humanity already. All you need is a pure heart and a desire to establish the connection. The rest you can learn from a book or a seminar.

Just as you can speak with individual beings in the Akashic records, so you can speak with God himself, too. Yes, you can. It is an interesting exercise, which will improve your sensitivity toward the different energies, to ask the same question to the Akashic records as a whole, to an individual master or teacher in the records, and to God. The number of questions you can ask is as endless as the universe itself.

In the previous chapters of this book, you read about the experiences my clients and I had with the Akashic records. In this chapter, I would like to deliver to you directly some beautiful messages I have received from the masters and from God. I ask you for your forgiveness for my lack of ability to adequately translate the incredible messages of these infinitely wise beings into the limited human language. I hope the following words will touch your heart and soul as they touched mine.

The Words of the Masters and Teachers of the Akashic Records

Question: Why are people afraid of death? Is there something to fear?

Answer: The fear of death is something relatively new on earth. Previous cultures accepted death calmly and even celebrated it, because they knew what it means to die—an end to one story, the return to the spirit family, and the beginning of a new story. When you finish a beautiful book, you sometimes mourn its ending, but then you remember all the wonderful scenes you read—all the scary, the romantic, the exciting, and the happy ones. It leaves a pleasant, warm feeling in your chest, and even though you will never forget this beautiful book, you are soon after looking forward to starting a new one. So, to let the physical body die means to get the chance of a new adventure.

In older cultures, people were able to connect to their deceased loved ones, so the separation was not so abrupt, tragic, or sad. For many reasons, some time ago, a great amount of knowledge was lost and hidden from the people, and the Dark Ages on earth began, and people were left to believe that death is the end of the journey. Some believed that it was only earthworms that were looking forward to them, and others feared hell (aren't these two options actually the same?). In truth, death is just one of the many stops on your soul's journey. People are afraid of the unknown, so they fear death because they do not understand it. People also fear the stories they have been told about death—the stories of a judgment day (how can you have a judgment day, which implies an end of times, when time does not exist?), the stories of an unforgiving God, the stories of atheism that after death is just the nothingness. These are terrible things to look forward to. No wonder people are terrified of dying. But interestingly, mostly young people are afraid of death. The older a person gets, the more s/he comes to terms with the inevitability of death; memories of the beyond start creeping in that give one hope and a warm feeling. Many are sad to leave their loved ones behind but are also looking forward to going back to peace. Earth has not been a peaceful place for a long time, and death has been one of the main methods to achieve it.

When people understand the real meaning of death, they will not be afraid anymore. The fear of death is a huge one for humanity, and once this fear is removed, many of your shackles will fall off, and you will awaken. So, let us tell you about death.

The soul does not die. One lifetime is for the soul like one movie that it has written and is now actually filming (adjustments can be done to the script, but once the camera is rolling, it is generally quite difficult, however not impossible). Some movies are comedies, some movies are romantic, and some movies are horrors. Each movie genre has its fan base. The special thing about the real-life movies is that they are usually very cathartic. Almost always, something happens to the hero (you) that transforms them forever. The movie has a beginning, a middle, and an end. So does the story of your life and your physical body. But once the physical body is shed, the soul remains. Actually, the soul barely feels the moment of death. Birth is usually much more traumatic for the soul than death is, because when born, your soul has to squeeze into the physical body, but when the body dies, the soul returns to its expanded state (a much more pleasant transition). Most people really enjoy the moment of death. It is a moment of liberation and of returning home from your travels. We of course do not mean that the suffering before death, which some people go through, is enjoyable. The suffering is definitely no fun, but it also has a meaning. Remember—everything that happens to you is to serve you and your soul. There is *nothing* that is outside of spirit, thus nothing can happen that does not serve the spirit. However, it is of course possible to leave the body without making it go through a painful experience. Many cultures, even in present earth days, practice conscious death and death at will. This is also, for example, how Jesus left the earth plane when his time came. This, however (and by no coincidence), is very tightly linked to a very spiritual life dedicated to self-development and growth of the soul.

You need not be afraid of death, dear ones. You will be fine when your moment comes. Your loved ones who have left the physical plane before you are fine too. Even though death in most cases means finally getting the relief of leaving a life of suffering, no soul is rushing to leave earth too soon. No one incarnated in a life to end this life. Life on earth, the chance to experience the physical reality, the opportunity to work through your karmic debts, the possibility to learn and grow—these are precious gifts that should not be rejected lightly. If you, however, decide to take your own life, you will not be judged afterward. You will only be loved, because your extreme suffering and loneliness made you take such a desperate step. The only being that might judge you is you, so do not take this lightly; you are your worst critic. However, once your soul recovers on the spirit side, it will reincarnate again and will repeat similar life situations until it manages to successfully go through the tests. There are no wrong decisions, but some decisions can lead you on a more joyful ride, while others might cause you extra pain. It is your choice which path you will take. It has always been your choice. And you have always known what you need to do to choose the right path for you.

Note from the author: as a hypnotherapist, I have had many hypnosis clients who experience a regression in a past life with me. We almost always also experience the moment of death from the past life. I have not had a client so far who did not enjoy it. It always feels like a liberation, like a pleasant sigh, like finally letting go of a heavy burden that you were not even aware you were carrying around.

Once I had a client who contemplated ending his life (which he told me afterward). In the regression session, he saw two past lives where he did manage to kill himself. After each death, he regretted deeply his choice and promised himself to do better next time. Each next life was getting more and more difficult; the lessons were getting more and more severe. If you reject a gift from God (like life), you need to prove that you *really* want it back. This time, my client took the spiritual path and was working on resolving his issues. When he saw that what he was contemplating doing now he had already done, and it did not lead at all to the desired liberation, he realized that this time he had to choose differently. He did not want to suffer from tormenting regrets after death, and he did not want to be pulled by the karmic wheel into an even grimmer next life. There is no way out of existence. The only way is up.

Question: What is positive and negative energy?

Answer: There is no positive and no negative energy. This is just how things look from your point of view; from ours, it is all one. Energy is energy; existence is existence. There are only different understandings of the same thing. When a thing is used to do harm, it can be seen as negative; when something is used to do the opposite of harm, it is seen as positive. And yet, who is to say what harm really is? There are no purely positive and purely negative things, as the consequences and the ripples in the universe are endless. The universe does not aim toward being positive or good. The universe aims at balance, at harmony. There is one middle point, one zero point, one zero field, and a deviation from it is seen as positive or as negative, but the aim is the balance, the lack of positive or negative, not the domination of one over the other. That is why you need not focus on being good, on being positive, on being always happy. You should focus on being balanced, on being in harmony with yourself and the universe. When you are in your middle, in your center, in your zero point, then your vision will not be tainted by the ideas of positive or negative. And remember, there cannot be positive without the negative and vice versa. That is why a big wave of positive thinking and action brings with it their negative counterparts. Do not strive to be purposely positive and to only do good. If it does not happen naturally, it means you are not in balance, but you are pushing yourself toward one of the extremes, and one extreme has its respective counterparts, and you will draw them, too, in the world, in order to restore the balance in your own universe. Focus instead on the balance within you and then your life will flow with ease, for there is no good or bad; there are simply different points of view. The Buddhist strive for nonattachment, the Christians strive for salvation, the indigenous peoples strive for harmony with nature. The key is to simply be in harmony with yourself, the world, and the universe.

Question: Can you resolve a situation with a person or life circumstances by finding out what happened in a past life?

Answer: The knowledge about the past life can help you understand the present. Sometimes simply knowing what the triggering situation was can be enough to resolve the issue you are struggling with. However, other times, remembering the circumstances is just the first step on your healing journey. It is also possible that knowing will not bring you any benefits or might even hurt you. In these cases, no information about a past life will be given by us. One way or another, if you need to know, you will receive the information, and the information will help the healing process.

It is time, dear children, that you remember. You have lived in the shadows for too long. You have been shielded from knowing, because knowing would have overwhelmed you, but now you are ready. You are now strong and wise enough to know and to deal with this knowledge. It might not be easy to see what you have done in a past life; you might feel sick to your stomach by this other person you see in your past life, but did you not have moments even in this life of which you are ashamed, and you would prefer they rather never happened? You need to heal and integrate and forgive the past. You need to love yourself in your entirety so you can achieve completeness and step into your full power of oneness.

Question: Why do we carry over energetic patterns from past lives?

Answer: You do not carry it over. Everything happens at the same time in the universe. If something, some pattern, is influencing you strongly in your current life, it is because it is happening at the same time in another of your lives. All your soul parts are connected, just like all your body organs are connected. Similarly, when one part of your body gets ill, the whole body feels it; thus, when an aspect of you is experiencing some kind of pain this influences you too. The way to heal yourself is to heal your whole self. You cannot heal only your current life without influencing your other reincarnations at the same time—and vice versa. You have not carried over energy from a past life; the "past" life is happening right now and is influencing you right now, and if you do not enjoy the pattern, you need to / can change it.

Many times, people who are into self-help and self-improvement complain that they have cleared some issue, but then it resurfaces again. This is so because this issue has not been healed on all levels of existence. A complete healing occurs when you have no recollection of the issue, when it no longer exists in your universe—in any of your versions and lives. Similarly, a complete recovery of your body is when your body has no memory—no scar left, just like before, with no trace of the health issue. In this exact way, when you have healed something completely, it will disappear from the universe like a scar that healed. It might remain as a memory, but it will not remain as a wound anymore.

Question: What is the difference between talking to God and to you, dear masters and teachers?

Answer: What is the difference between summer and winter? What is the difference between day and night? Between the sun and the moon? The mountain and the valley? It is huge. So is the difference between connecting to us and connecting directly to God. Our role is simply to assist you on your way back to God. God's role is simply to be. God simply is. He does not want to push you forward or to push you backward. God simply is. God is all the action in one and at the same time all the stillness in one. We ourselves understand the stillness of God and also strive for it, like you do. We are not yet God; we are not yet stillness; we are not yet the oneness. And at the same time, we are. For it all simultaneously exists and does not. All realities and possibilities exist at the same time. We are able to tune into specific frequencies. God is all the frequencies.

We still have desires and wishes and hopes. We wish to see you free, and we have made ourselves available to you to teach you, guide you, and help you realize who you are. God, on the other hand, is free of any desires. God simply is. God knows. God is in no hurry. We are guilty of sometimes pushing you to grow, to evolve faster, to awaken from the dream. Oh, how many more wonders await you, dear ones. God has created this beautiful garden for us to explore and rejoice in. It is not his job to personally tend it. He breathed life in us so we can do it ourselves. We are all in this together, and we are all in God.

Question: What do we need to do to help heal the world?

Answer: The events of the world are like the tidal waves of the ocean. The world does not need healing. Just like nobody of you needs to be healed. It is all perfect the way it is. You are perfect the way you are. The world is perfect the way it is. The way of the flow, of the nonresistance, of the no-fighting is the way through. You cannot stop the ocean waves, but you can learn to ride them. That which you resist persists. Give your attention to that which you want to see grow; take away your attention from that which you want to see no more in your life. It is like tending a garden; the crops you spend more time tending will be the ones that thrive the most. Create around you the world you dream to live in. Anything you do should be done from a place of "The world is whole, the world is perfect, people are whole, and people are perfect." You do not need to try to heal anything or anyone, as they are not broken and in need of being fixed. Anything you do should be done from a place of "I want to spread love. I want to see people smile. I want to make people happy." Anything you do should be done from a place of "It is all perfect. Let us simply share with one another our perfection and rejoice in in."

The Words of God

One night a man had a dream.
He dreamed he was walking along the beach with the Lord.

In the sand he saw the path of his life and
every step along the way that he took.
In the sand there were two sets of footprints—one
belonging to him, and the other belonging to the Lord.
However, he noticed that many times along the path
of his life there was only one set of footprints.
He also noticed that it happened at the very
lowest and saddest times of his life.
This really bothered him, and he questioned the Lord about it.

"Lord, I was told you are always there for me and walk side
by side with me my whole life. But I couldn't help but notice
that during the most troublesome times in my life there is

only one set of footprints in the sand. I don't understand why when I needed you the most you would leave me."

The Lord replied, "My precious child, I love you and would never leave you. I have always walked along you during your life and have supported you and cheered for you at every single moment of your life. However, during the times of trial and suffering, when you see only one set of footprints in the sand—these are not yours, they are mine. You were not left alone, my child—it was then that I carried you."

—Author Unknown

Question: Are you the only God there is?

God's Answer: I am who I am. I am the beginning and the end, the alpha and the omega. I am the serpent who bites its tail. I am. I am in you, and you are in me. I am everything that is, and everything is you. There is nothing that is left to be something separate.

Me: Aren't you lonely? What is the goal of your existence then?

God: I couldn't be happier and more entertained. I have everything I could ever wish for. I have you, my child. The goal of my existence is your existence, and the goal of your existence is my praise.

Me: Who created you?

God: I have always been. I have no beginning, and I have no end. I was not created, and I cannot be destroyed. I am currently awake, and so all life exists. When I fall asleep, life will cease to exist. This is the closest I can get to not existing. And when I awaken again in the next cycle, life will reawaken with me again. But do not worry, dear children, my days are very, very long, and when the wheel turns and I start feeling tired, you will start feeling tired too. We will all want to cease to exist at the same time.

Me: I thought time does not exist.

God: What is time? Time does not exist, but different states of being do. When one state of being exists, then all others cease to exist.

Me: Don't you get tired of watching people do the same mistakes over and over again?

God: I never get tired of watching you. Does a loving mother ever get tired of being with her dear kids? And you never repeat the same mistake twice; no two moments in existence are the same.

Me: Do you feel sad when you see people suffering?

God: I feel every single ounce of what you feel. The whole universe feels what you feel. When you suffer, we all suffer. When you rejoice, we all rejoice. We are all one. None is separate from the other. We are all interwoven in one another. But I have the capacity to "endure" enormous amounts of "suffering" and "joy" as well as everything in between. I simply call this *existence.*

Me: Are there other Gods like you?

God: I have no ends, and I have no beginnings. I am all that is.

Me: Can I see beyond you?

God: Yes, you can look beyond me. Make a full circle, and then you will be back to looking into your own eyes.

Me: God, why did you create the universe? Were you simply bored?

God: I did not. It was just a thought I had, and my thought became reality, and I saw that it was good, and I kept it.

Me: So, you were not bored?

God: Bored of what? Of existing? I exist now too. Nothing has changed in that respect.

Me: So, you were not lonely?

God: Lonely? I have all life within me. I have all the potentials of all the endless possibilities of universes. I am life itself. How can life be lonely?

Me: So, you did not create the universe intentionally? It was an accident?

God: It was not an accident. It was a thought I had, but it was a controlled thought. Like your monks learn to meditate and control their thoughts, so can I, or rather they learn to be like me.

Me: Was this your first thought of a universe?

God: Time is an illusion. There is not first or last. It all exists in the now.

Me: So, you are like a supercomputer that is computing (thinking) many thoughts in parallel?

God: There are moments in existence when I am thinking an endless number of thoughts at the same "time," and there are other moments of existence when I have a single thought, and then there are moments of existence when I have no thoughts. These are all potentials (thinking and not thinking) that exist at the same "time" within me.

Me: Did someone create you? Are you a thought of another God?

God: I have no beginnings and no ends. I am the serpent that bites its tail. No others exist but me. I am all that is. All encompassing. All seeing. All knowing.

Question: Why did you create the archangels?

God's Answer: I did not create them. Creation cannot be forced or ordered to happen. I invited them, and they created themselves out of me. It was their decision, not mine. Each one of you has free will. The number of the archangels changes with time, because their souls decide to come in and out of existence. (Archangel) Michael, for example, is a very dedicated one. He wants to be helping you and will not leave this existence without you under his (winged) arms.

Me: What is the difference between you and the archangels?

God: I am them, and they are I, but they are different expressions of my I. They are expressions who decided to manifest in order to be seen and recognized and in order to be of service to existence.

Me: Can you give orders to the archangels?

God: I do not give orders. Each one of you knows what the right thing to do is. This feeling of knowing in you is my will, my invitation, my desire. But it is your decision if you will follow my will or yours. I have no attachment to the choices you make. Your freedom makes me happy. Each higher dimension has control over the one under it. The question is if it wants to exercise this control or not. The lower you go on the levels and dimensions, the more control is exercised; the higher you go, the less control is exercised. You are still living in a dimension that wants to exercise and needs a lot of control, and it is OK for it to be so. But know that it does not have to be so. The higher you go on the dimensions, the less you will need or want to exercise control over those around you, above you, or below you, for you will not need control in order to have what you want and to feel fulfilled.

Question: Why is there so much suffering in the world? So many hungry and sick people?

God's Answer: It is scarier to be hungry in spirit than in body; it is scarier for your spirit to be sick than for your body to be so. The wounds of the body you can see, but the wounds of the soul hurt much more. The illusion of this material reality has you in its grasp, but you can easily free yourself if you so wish. Do not focus on the sick and hungry in body; focus on the sick and hungry in spirit, for when their spirit is healed, their bodies will be too. Bodily sickness is part of your experience in this reality, like rain is part of the rainy season in the Amazon forest. One will not be the same without the other. It was your choice to experience this way of existence, this reality. However, this does not mean you should look at people's suffering as their fault or as their choice. You are to have compassion for their pain, for this pain is real. The pain comes from the unknowing, from the strong illusion that has the person in its clasp. Do help those who are suffering, for their pain is my pain, and it is your pain too. Like a dream can make you cry, so your earthly experience can make you hurt. It is all a dream within the dream within the dream, but they are all real, and you are waking up from one dream to awaken into the other, until you awaken for one last time and then wake up as the all-that-is, as me. Help those who you see suffering, and your own suffering will be reduced. Dear child, have always compassion toward the pains of your brothers and sisters. The fear of a child of the monster in the dark is just as strong, regardless of if there is a monster in the dark or no. Hug the child, gift her your love, and promise her that it will be all right, and then the light will come into the darkness, and the child will see that there was never a monster there.

Question: What is the role of the church as an organization, and why does it portray an image of a God who punishes us for our sins? Are you such a God?

God's Answer: This question creates excruciating pain in me. I would never hurt you. I would never punish you. I would never harm you. It pains me you could think such a thing. It pains me to see the suffering this is creating in you. I love you, and you are the goal of my existence. I exist, and so do you; you exist, and so I do. You are my children, and I exist for you and you for me. We are one. Forever. In my eyes, you are perfect. You need not do anything to achieve my love. You have it by the definition of your existence. You need not be afraid that you will anger me with your thoughts, deeds, words, or feelings, for I know who you truly are deep in your heart. If you are angry with me or feeling revengeful or fearful, it is because you have lost your connection to me, because you cannot feel me in you anymore, and you think I abandoned you. This was the original role of the church—to remind people of that feeling, to bring back in their hearts the memory of me, the feeling of love and being loved. Do not put your focus on the few church people who have themselves lost their connection to me; think rather about all those who have dedicated their hearts, lives, and souls to my service and have taken to heart their mission—the mission to hold the light, to keep the flame burning, to remind people where they come from, what their origin is, to remind them that they are not alone, to tell them that they are loved and cared for and provided for. And as you need rules that the police keep, people need spiritual rules. This is the role of the church. Some people don't need the control anymore, but others do, and this is OK.

A child first gets scared when he thinks he has lost his parents in the crowd. Then after some time, if the parents do not appear, the child starts being angry at the parents, and then after some time, the child doubts that the parents ever existed or loved him at all. Each one of you is at a different stage of forgetting that we were once one. You should know that I am always there for you, but you should also know that I am keeping my distance because you asked me to. You wanted to be independent and play the game of earth. And I saw that this game was beneficial for you, and I left you play it. But I will never leave you feeling lost, for I am always here for you. Know that every time, when you ask for my help and for my love, it is immediately there for you. I am always loving you, encouraging you, being there for you, and rejoicing at your victories. I am in everything and everyone, so welcome me no matter how I come into your life.

Question: Why are there different religions in the world—religions that talk about one God and religions that talk about many gods?

Answer: Why are there people with different skin colors in the world? Why are there so many different types of flowers? Why are not all planets the same? Diversity is the beauty of life, child. The world is an expression of me, and I have so many different faces, facets, and forms. The beauty and magic of life lies within the myriad of possibilities of expression there are. And just like a hundred different poets will describe one flower in a hundred different ways, so have the different religions described me in different ways. Some have seen the core of me and have described me as one thing (which I am not; I am all things that exist); some have described and named different aspects of me and have dedicated their lives to studying these separate aspects (which I am also not, for one part of me cannot be separated from the others, for it is all one). In order to understand me, you need to know all parts of me and me as a whole, which, dear child, you are doing via your exploration throughout the universe. What you call enlightenment in your plane of existence is understanding fully my expression in this plane of existence; then you can continue to the next one. It is, however, important to know, dear child, that you do *not* need to know me in my entirety. You are part of me, and I am within you; when you so choose, you can immediately return to me and merge fully back into me, and then and only then, you will know me.

A hidden question within your question is, "Which religion is the right one?" I know that from your perspective, they might be saying contradictory things, and they are at times. However, know that no human can know, understand, and explain God fully and correctly. The beings who founded the different religions put their own flavor and understanding into it. A person is as flawed as an unpolished piece of coal and as perfect as the diamond within. Do not judge your brothers and sisters of different religions. You should rather join your efforts and try to combine your different understandings in order to receive a fuller picture. However, you do not need to. You do not need somebody else to tell you who I am. You *know* who I am. You are me, and I am within you. You know me, dear child. Trust your inner knowing and trust that the inner knowing of another is their way of viewing the piece of me that they are embodying.

Question: What do we need to do to help heal the world?

Answer: Dear child, the world is I. Why do you think you need to heal me?

Me: People are suffering.

God: Indeed, people are experiencing the strong illusion of separation and suffering. But it is only an illusion. And it has been your choice to indulge yourself in your illusion. When your children play soldiers, do you stop them, or do you leave them to have fun? I know that you are just playing, and you know it too. Just sometimes you get so engulfed in the game that you forget for a while it is just a game. And this is when the game is most enjoyable—when you forget it is a game, and you in truth turn into the pirate, the princes, the villain, the hero. I do not want you to suffer, dear ones; you do not want to suffer either. You just want to play different games and try on different suits, and I let you do it. If you, however, ever feel you are suffering, you can follow this three-step process:

1.   Stop and breathe.
2.   Call upon me and tell me about your pain. I want to hear all the details.
3.   Let it all go and let me deal with it for you.

I love you. You are flesh of my flesh. You are breath of my breath. You are spark of my essence. You and I are one.

Question: What do you want me to know at this present time?

Answer: I want you to never forget that I am always there for you. I don't want you to ever think that you are alone. I want you to remember how cared for you are—by me and by your other brothers and sisters within creation. I want you to always feel at home no matter where you are, for you are always in my home. I want you to be brave and to go after your dreams, for your dreams are good, and I wish for them to come into reality. I want you to be kind to yourself and others, for each one of you is my child, and each one of you is me. I want you to love and respect yourself, for in that way, you love and respect me, for I am you and you are within me.

I love you. I bless you. I care for you. I cherish you. I look after you, dear child. Never forget it. And never forget that I am not far but so, so very close. I am the voice in your head, the beating of your heart, the wind in the trees, the colors of the rainbow, and the smile on people's faces. I am everything and everyone.

I am all.
I am omnipotent and omnipresent.
I am you.
You are as I am.
Amen.

ABOUT THE AUTHOR

Dr. Yana Mileva was born in Bulgaria but lived half of her life in Germany. She loves both countries and she loves travelling the rest of the world too. Despite her obvious inclination toward the natural sciences (she has a PhD in computer science), the author started working with the spiritual, invisible world from a very early age. Her interest in the unknown and unseen drove her to go through and master many modalities—energy healing, card reading, hypnosis, psychological coaching, meditation. She explored different religions and worked with different spiritual masters. Yana found her home in the work with the Akashic records. Since 2011, she has been consciously in contact with the masters and teachers of the Akashic records; unconsciously, she says they were in contact all her life. Since 2013, the author has been giving Akashic records readings and working with clients to convey to them the words of the masters and that which is written in the Akashic records. Since 2014, Yana has been a certified Akashic records teacher and has since then been spreading the wisdom and love of the masters.

Printed in the United States
by Baker & Taylor Publisher Services